I Just Let Life Rain Down on Me

SEAGULL
BOOKS
•
CELEBRATING
40 YEARS

THE GERMAN LIST

RAHEL LEVIN VARNHAGEN

I Just Let Life Rain Down on Me

Letters and Reflections

Selected and Translated
by Peter Wortsman

LONDON NEW YORK CALCUTTA

This publication has been supported by
a grant from the Goethe-Institut India.

Seagull Books, 2024

The first edition of Rahel Varnhagen's letters, curated by her husband Karl
August, were published posthumously as *Rahel: Ein Buch des Andenkens für
ihre Freunde*, 3 VOLS (Berlin, 1834).

This initial selection of letters was more recently expanded to a six-volume
edition published by Wallstein Verlag:
Rahel: Ein Buch des Andenkens für ihre Freunde, 6 VOLS (Barbara Hahn ed.)
(Göttingen, Wallstein Verlag, 2011).
The translator has consulted this new edition of the letters and thanks
Wallstein and Barbara Hahn for the same.

First published in English translation by Seagull Books, 2024
Translator's foreword and English translation © Peter Worstman, 2024

ISBN 978 1 80309 336 9

British Library Cataloguing-in-Publication Data
A catalogue record for this book is available from the British Library

Typeset by Seagull Books, Calcutta, India
Printed and bound in the USA by Integrated Books International

What else, in essence, is the human being but a question posed?

Rahel Levin Varnhagen

To the memory of my grandmother,
Julia, and my mother, Dora,
and to the ongoing inspiration of my wife, Claudie,
my sister, Evelyn, my daughter, Aurélie,
my nieces Julie, Alie and Lia,
and all the brilliant women in my life.

—Peter Worstman

CONTENTS

IV

GRAPPLING WITH GOETHE AND OTHER CONTEMPORARY
AUTHORS OF NOTE, AND OTHER LITERARY REFLECTIONS

V

LETTERS TO AND RECOLLECTIONS OF CONVERSATIONS WITH
KARL AUGUST VARNHAGEN VON ENSE

VI

REFLECTIONS

VII

APHORISMS

RETURN TO SENDER

A Translator's Foreword

A letter always seemed to me like immortality because it is the mind alone without corporeal friend.

Emily Dickinson

Now that the terse text message with its streamlined syntax has all but supplanted the email, the handwritten pen-and-ink letter must seem as anachronistic to the contemporary mindset as prehistoric handprints on cave walls. Like a prayer, the personal letter is a passionate declaration directed from an *I* to a *thou*, replete with pathos and longing, sans all the holy hyperbole. In parts poetic but not a poem, in parts prosaic but not an essay, a letter is pure writing for writing's sake. Scholars peruse the letters of prominent people to better understand their actions and accomplishments, and in the case of poets and writers, for the insights their letters offer into the matrix of their more formal works. Only very rarely is the letter prized as a literary form in its own right.

Women have been among the most adept and prolific letter writers, at least in part because they have long been relegated to the domestic sphere and largely excluded from writing and publishing anything else. One of the most illustrious among female letter writers in the Western canon is Marie de Rabutin-Chantal, aka Madame de Sévigné, the Marquise de Sévigné (1626–96). Her evocative missives to her daughter Françoise-Marguerite de Sévigné, Comtesse de Grignan (1646–1705) are considered classics of seventeenth-century French literature.

In the German-speaking world, Rahel Varnhagen von Ense, née Levin (1771–1833), the illustrious German Jewish literary-salon hostess from Berlin, is likewise renowned for her letters, over 10,000 of which she penned in the course of her life to more than 300 recipients, including princes, philosophers, poets, family members and the family cook; some 6,000 of her letters are still extant today. Rahel expressed no false modesty about her letters. In a letter to a friend, she wrote:

> [T]hese bon mots taken from a heap of letters and from a few diaries—collected by Varnhagen—are the product of silent, long-lived, long-ignored pains, tears, suffering, brooding; the fruit of solitude and consequence of breaks in the never-ending ennui. Pearls compressed for a half century and spit up out of a stormy human soul, treasures of the kind dredged from the deep [. . .][1]

---

1 See 'Words are pearls compressed for a half century and spit up out of a stormy human soul' (To Antonie von Horn) in this volume, pp. 110–11; here, p. 111.

Written with a wink at posterity, clearly conceived as compositions worth preserving, collected and published after her passing by her husband Karl August Varnhagen von Ense (1785–1858), they constitute a singular contribution to German literature. She summed up her epistolary aesthetic in a letter to a friend:

> I do want a letter to be a portrait of the moment in which it is written; and it succeeds, in my estimation, principally depending on how much it accords with the ideal artistic demands of the form, demands the letter writer must take into account, but blind adherence to which yields an affected and empty result.[2]

The poignant lyricism of Rahel's letters is all the more remarkable when we take into account that German was not her native tongue. The precocious oldest daughter of Levin Markus Cohen (1723–90), a jeweller, banker and businessman, and Chaie, née Moses (1742–1809), Rahel grew up speaking, reading and writing primarily Yiddish, a German dialect written in Hebrew letters, derogatively still referred to in her day as 'Juden-Deutsch' (Jews' German). The Levins were one of a little more than 300 prosperous Jewish families permitted to reside in Berlin, which at around 1800 comprised a mere one to two per cent of the total Jewish population of

---

2 See 'I do want a letter to be a portrait of the moment in which it was written' (To Konrad Engelbert Oelsner in Paris) in this volume, pp. 80–81; here, p. 81.

Prussia. The homes of Berlin's so-called 'Schutzjuden' (protected Jews), their number strictly regulated by the king, were a kind of neutral ground outside the grid of social constraints, where cultivated Christians and Jews engaged in a relatively free exchange of ideas.

Yet whereas her brothers were formally educated—the oldest, Markus Theodor (1772–1826) in business affairs; her younger brother, Ludwig Robert-Tornow (1778–1832), a poet and playwright, at the Französisches Gymnasium, a prestigious institution in Berlin founded by exiled French Huguenots—Rahel was home-schooled in German, French, piano and dance, disciplines deemed appropriate for girls and suitable to make them more marriageable. But from early on, Rahel bucked the cliché of the subservient female whose sole raison d'être is to make a good match, bear children and manage a household. An autodidact in literature and philosophy, among other areas of interest, she became an avid reader of and commentator on the works of her contemporaries, with a particular appreciation for the poetry of Johann Wolfgang von Goethe (1749–1832). Among the only texts of hers published in her lifetime were commentaries on Goethe excerpted from her correspondence with her husband and selected and issued by him. But the best of her letters are more than mere commentary, they are declarations concerning every aspect of life formulated in a voice as fresh and original as that of any of the recognized poets and thinkers of her day.

'Your letters are not really written, they are living people [. . .]. They read as if they were spoken aloud,' declared a friend, the German writer and political thinker Friedrich von Gentz (1764–1832).[3] Another friend with whom she carried on an extensive correspondence, the German Jewish physician and thinker David Veit (1771– 1814), opined: 'In her letters [. . .] every word always reads as if she had just now invented it.'

Rahel herself put it this way: '[O]ur language is our lived life; I invented mine for my own purposes, I was less able than many others to make use of preconceived turns of phrase, which is why mine are often clumsy, and in all respects faulty, but always true.'[4]

Idiosyncratic in her orthography, punctuation and grammar, she took considerable liberties with sentence structure, teased out and toyed with the meaning of familiar terms, coined new words and spun run-on sentences that hone close to the erratic contour of consciousness—all of which often makes her writing difficult to fathom and a formidable challenge to translate. With tongue-in-cheek humour, for instance, she coined the word *Witzschlag*, a composite of the German words *Witz* (wit) and *Blitzschlag* (flash of lightning), thus 'a bolt of wit'. And with a self-deprecatory irony, she

---

3 From a letter addressed to Rahel, dated 2 March 1803.

4 From a letter written in 1801 to Georg Wilhelm Bokelmann, a Danish Hamburg businessman whom she met in Paris and with whom she had a brief flirtation.

REPLY TO SENDER • *xviii*

invented another word, *Scheinschreiben* (pseudo-writing), to refer to her own, in her words, 'clumsy, and in all respects faulty, but always true' prose.

It is as if the nib of her pen were linked directly to the tip of her tongue.

The spoken word was Rahel's real forte, and her real passion was socializing with a select coterie of like-minded souls who gathered at her digs to indulge in a free and open exchange of ideas. She hosted literary salons during two distinct periods in her life, the first begun as a precocious teen, starting when she was 19, in her parents' house, from 1790 to 1806, the year Napoleon defeated the Prussians and invaded Berlin; the second, together with her husband Karl August, from 1819 until her death in 1833.

As she put it in a letter to a sometime friend, the German Romantic poet and writer Clemens Brentano (1778–1842):[5]

As far back as I can remember, I have always had a boundless love for socializing with friends, and am quite certain that I was so conceived and so equipped by nature. My presence of mind and quick-wittedness permit me to grasp, respond and discuss. Endowed

---

5 Some of the very same German Romantic poets, including Clemens Brentano, whom she welcomed into her salon as young, up-and-coming talents, would later betray her trust, expressly excluding Jews and women, among other undesirables, from their own old boys' club, the Christlich-Deutsche Tischgesellschaft (The German Christian Table Society), founded in 1811.

with a keen sense of human nature and the nature of all relationships, a sense of wit and seriousness [. . .], humble as I am, I let down my guard by speaking; I can keep quiet for a very long time, love all manifestations of humanity and can suffer almost all people.[6]

While most Jewish men of means, like her father, were solely associated with and essentially reduced to their pecuniary worth, their wives and daughters functioned as relatively free agents, rare caged birds with an exotic appeal. Rahel's brilliant repartee made her a prized intellectual catalytic agent for those who flocked to her salon. Held in the highest esteem by her contemporaries—'the brightest woman in Europe', according to German historian Leopold von Ranke (1795–1886);[7] German Jewish poet Heinrich Heine (1797–1856) upped the ante, calling her 'the most quick-witted woman in the universe';[8] and the German author Jean Paul (1763–1825) lauded her ability to 'treat life in a poetic fashion, and life returns the favour'.[9]

---

6 From a letter written over four days, 1–4 August 1813; excerpted and translated from Rahel Levin Varnhagen, *Rahel: Ein Buch des Andenkens für ihre Freunde*, 6 VOLS (Barbara Hahn ed.) (Göttingen: Wallstein, 2011), VOL. 2, p. 511.

7 Quoted in Dorothee Nolte, *Ich liebe unendlich Gesellschaft: Rahel Varnhagen, Lebensbild einer Salonière* (Berlin: Eulenspiegel, 2021), p. 5.

8 Quoted in Von Harro Zimmermann, 'Meisterin der Kommunikation', *Deutschlandfunk* (12 June 2011) (available online: rebrand.ly/ypwv6ip; last accessed: 30 October 2023).

9 From a letter to Rahel, dated 6 November 1800, written soon after meeting her for the first time; quoted in Dieter Lamping, 'Ein

Those who met her for the first time were oftentimes flabbergasted at the apparent dichotomy between her plain appearance and her sparkling wit. 'Then the aging, perhaps never beautiful, stooped, fairy-like, not to say witch-like, woman started speaking, and I was bewitched,' recalled Austrian writer and playwright Franz Grillparzer (1791– 1872). 'My fatigue dissipated, or rather gave way to intoxication. She spoke and spoke until round about midnight [. . .] Never in my life have I heard a person speak better and in a more interesting manner.'[10]

'The beautiful thing about Rahel's spirit was her original take on things, according to which she shaped her opinions,' wrote another friend, the writer, publisher, composer and social activist Bettina von Arnim (1785–1859). 'She was tolerant where others were quick to condemn, and she tasted the salt in that which others dismissed as the burnt ash of a consumed life. To be just is a godly art.'[11]

Small of stature, ill-proportioned, ungainly, lacking the physical allure and charm by which women have long been and are still judged, all the while abjuring any false modesty, she was nevertheless convinced of her own intellectual

---

"weiblicher Mensch": Rahel erklärt sich' in *Rahel Varnhagen: Ich lasse das Leben auf mich regnen* (Cologne: ebersbach & simon, 2021).

10 Franz Grillparzer, *Selbstbiographie* in *Sämtliche Werke: Ausgewählte Briefe, Gespräche, Berichte*, 4 VOLS (Munich: Carl Hanser, 1961–65), VOL. 4, p. 137.

11 From a letter addressed to Rahel's grieving husband Karl August Varnhagen von Ense, dated 29 September 1838.

prowess—'I am as singular as the greatest soul on earth. The greatest artist, philosopher or poet has nothing on me. We are made of the same stuff.'[12]

Well aware of the worth of her words, as early as 1794 she wrote to remind her brother Markus who, as the oldest male heir, was anointed head of the family following her father's death: 'Save my letters, for they are my journals; I cannot write it twice, I do everything on the spur of the moment. No impression must be lost.'[13] As the lightning bolt is to the lightbulb, her letters burst the constraints of ordinary communication, flooding the recipient with insight. Or as she phrased her intent in a letter dated 1 July 1800 to Wilhelmine von Boye in Stralsund:

> Adieu!—and when I die—I will gather up all my letters—by devious means—hoping to retrieve them from all my friends and acquaintances [. . .] It will make for an original story and very poetic. [. . .] This, Boye, I demand of you as a duty. [. . .] It is not, I think, too much to ask of a friend.[14]

---

12 See 'The greatest artist, philosopher or poet has nothing on me' in this volume, pp. 37–38; here, p. 38.

13 From a letter to Markus dated 8–10 August 1794; quoted in Beatrix Langner, '1547 Seiten Familienkorrespondenz', *Deutschlandfunk* (17 February 2010) (available online: https://rebrand.ly/b0uhuz2; last accessed: 30 October 2023).

14 *Rahel: Ein Buch des Andenkens für ihre Freunde* (Barbara Hahn ed.), VOL. 1, p. 215.

In her letters, Rahel played language riffs as others play musical instruments.

Here she is expounding on the nature of the poet: 'A poet is a person in whom all strings on which experience plays are plucked, whereupon they vibrate; but what of those in whom such strings are absent!'[15]

Here she is extoling dance:

> Yes, I waltz. For the past five Mondays we've established a dance hour at home—ever since the third session I kicked up my legs and started waltzing, and not half badly; and do you think a girl can keep a steady head with all that unwholesome twisting and turning?—though I can't quite take the sensual pleasure in it that most people do, half of them picturing it as perilous to their health, the other half as sheer heavenly delight [. . .][16]

Here she is assessing her linguistic failings:

> Much as I resolve to pay heed to orthography while reading, I almost never manage, and if I do so at the very start of reading something, I don't really read, but just see the way the words are written; but I soon grow tired of it and return to reading; this makes me feel terribly sad for myself, and the simplest soul can learn more than me, and it would be insufferable if I did not find some small consolation in not blaming the faulty

---

15 See 'The poet' in this volume, p. 14.
16 See 'Yes, I waltz' in this volume, pp. 29–30; here, p. 29.

side of my brain, but rather acknowledging that it is the good side that ill serves me. [. . .]¹⁷

And here she is figuratively dissecting the self: 'A person can, like a book, be torn to shreds.'

*

The author whose extensive correspondence immediately comes to mind when considering Rahel's letters is Franz Kafka (1883–1924). Though Kafka mastered German and wrote in the clear, bureaucratic manner of a doctor or lawyer, both treat language as a malleable material to express a mindset hors norme, a consciousness rooted in a uniquely Jewish mix of intellectual acuity and profound emotional insecurity.

'But I myself cannot keep on living,' Kafka wrote to a friend,

since I have never really lived, I remained mud, never managed to make the spark of life in me ignite into a flame, but only managed to use it to shed a little light on my cadaver. It will make for a funny kind of funeral, in that the writer, that insubstantial something, passed on his old cadaver, a cadaver since day one, to the grave.¹⁸

---

17 See 'My incorrect writing' in this volume, pp. 25–28; here, p. 25.
18 Franz Kafka, 'A Writer's Quandary' in *Konundrum* (Peter Wortsman ed. and trans.) (New York: Archipelago Books, 2016), pp. 47–51; here, p. 49.

Rahel, who died a half century before Kafka was born, could just as well have written the above words. And as Kafka famously vented his spleen in a letter to his father, so did Rahel, too, spill her guts in a tell-all accusatory letter to her mother, with whom she maintained strained relations:

> Having levelled against me the easily refuted admonishment that I simply don't know what I want, you will, I trust, be so kind as to permit me to present my situation one last time! You know my age; but my heartfelt distress will forever remain a mystery to you. I am financially dependent on you: you alone could protect me and through your loving treatment grant me a sanctuary for my injured heart. This is how things stand for me now.[19]

Like Kafka, Rahel drew on her dreams and tapped her unconscious as a source of literary inspiration. 'I am much more wide awake in sleep,' she wrote to her husband.[20]

And just as posterity owes a debt of gratitude to Kafka's friend Max Brod for disobeying his express wishes to burn all his unpublished papers after his death, opting instead not only to preserve but also to tirelessly promote the man and his opus, so too are we beholden to Rahel's husband Karl August

---

19 See 'A letter of reckoning with Mother' in this volume, pp. 11–15; here, p. 11.

20 From a letter dated 23 May 1814; quoted in Barbara Hahn (ed.), *Im Schlaf bin ich wacher: Die Träume der Rahel Levin Varnhagen* (Munich: Luchterhand Literaturvlg, 1993).

Varnhagen von Ense, a German archivist, biographer, diplomat and soldier, who devoted the better part of his adult life as a quasi-apostle to building and bolstering her reputation. His admiration for Rahel bordered on adulation: 'I should like to live as your apostle,' he wrote to her,

> I spoke of you at Steffens' house, as the third glory of the Jewish nation, the first and second chronologically being Christ and Spinoza; [. . .] they accused me of idolatry, but Steffens was nevertheless delighted with my fervour.[21]

In her brilliant, albeit quirky, biography, *Rahel Varnhagen: The Life of a Jewish Woman* (1957), the German Jewish philosopher Hannah Arendt (1906–75) took Rahel's doting husband to task, unfairly I believe, for turning his wife into a marketable commodity, making her more palatable to the literate German-speaking public of his day by diluting the Jewish element, and to that end often obscuring the Jewish ancestry of a number of her correspondents. He did what he believed to be in her best interest, to spread the word to as wide a readership as possible, leaving it to future generations to flesh out a more complex profile.

✻

---

21 In a letter addressed to Rahel, dated 27 May 1810.

Posterity is hard pressed to balance Rahel's prickly mix of pride and prejudice as to her own cultural identity. In his book *The Pity of It All: A Portrait of Jews in Germany, 1743–1933* (2002), Israeli journalist Amos Elon glossed over Rahel's brilliance and reduced her to a simpering product of Jewish self-loathing:

> She hated her Jewish background and was convinced it had poisoned her life. For much of her adult life she was what would later be called self-hating. Her over-riding desire was to free herself from the shackles of her birth; since, as she thought, she had been 'pushed out of the world' by her origins, she was determined to escape them. [. . .] She considered her origins 'a curse, a slow bleeding to death'. The idea that as a Jew she was always required to be exceptional—and to go on proving it all the time—was repugnant to her. 'How wretched it is always to have to legitimize myself! That is why it is so disgusting to be a Jew.'[22]

But dare we condemn her stance in hindsight? Dare we judge what it meant to manoeuvre the tides of endemic prejudice and fleeting tolerance as a Jew in late-eighteenth- and early-nineteenth-century Prussia? She was hardly the only Jew in her day to feel a certain ambivalence about her ancestry and to resort to baptism as a survival tactic in an essentially

---

22 Amos Elon, *The Pity of It All: A Portrait of Jews in Germany, 1743–1933* (London: Penguin, 2003), p. 81.

hostile environment. The German Jewish philosopher Moses Mendelssohn (1729–86), a friend of the philosopher Immanuel Kant (1724–1804) and the playwright Gotthold Ephraim Lessing (1729–81), one of the first Jews to emerge from the isolation of the ghetto and make his mark in German culture as more than a moneylender, sought in his expression of faith a shaky compromise between Jewish orthodoxy and German assimilation. Though that compromise might have worked for him, it proved a strain on his progeny. Of Mendelssohn's six children, only two retained the Jewish faith. His oldest daughter Brendel, better known to posterity as Dorothea von Schlegel (1764–1839), a childhood friend of Rahel's, left her first husband Simon Veit and her father's faith to run off, convert and marry the German poet and philosopher Friedrich von Schlegel (1772–1829). Moses' grandson, the composer Felix Mendelssohn (1809–47), was baptized by his parents at age seven. The poet Heinrich Heine, another close friend of Rahel's, referred to his own baptismal certificate as his 'admission ticket into European culture'. Political writer and satirist Ludwig Börne, born Loeb Baruch (1786–1837), likewise opted for baptism as a passport to acceptance.

Despite the at-best tenuous accord between Germans and Jews over the more than 1,700 years of their cohabitation in German lands, a relationship disrupted time and again by onerous laws, persecution and outbreaks of violence, Germans and Jews established a certain entente that allowed for a cultural cross-fertilization. 'The German-speaking Jews and

their history are an altogether unique phenomenon,' affirms
Arendt, herself a product and case in point of that cultural
marriage, 'nothing comparable is to be found even in the other
areas of Jewish assimilation.'[23] Though himself hardly a friend
of the Jews, Martin Luther's translation of the Bible—completed in 1534, the first full translation of the Old and New
Testaments into German to reference not only the Latin
Vulgate, but also the original Hebrew and Greek texts—is
deemed by many to be the first work of modern German
literature. So, in a sense, the modern German mindset was
reconfigured, through Luther's lens, in the mirror image of the
ancient Semitic. Systemic prejudice, ongoing persecution and
reoccurring violence against the Jews in German lands notwithstanding, Germans and Jews have been simultaneously
harmonizing and hammering out their differences ever since.
The late nineteenth and mid-twentieth centuries saw the pin-
nacle and the nadir of that cultural dynamic. It would be
impossible to conceive of a Karl Marx, a Sigmund Freud, a
Franz Kafka, a Ludwig Wittgenstein or an Albert Einstein without the melding of Semitic Messianism and Teutonic idealism,
Jewish savvy and sechel (common sense), and strict German
syntax and clarity of thought. Depending on the tenor of the
times and the wavering attitude of local ecclesiastic and secular
authorities—tolerated and even feted by a tiny intellectual elite

23 Hannah Arendt, Preface to *Rahel Varnhagen: The Life of a Jewish Woman* (Richard Winston and Clara Winston trans, Barbara Hahn intro.) (New York: New York Review of Books, 2022), p. *xxiii*.

in periods of relative calm, reassuming their insidious role of scapegoat and reviled in periods of crisis—Jews remained by and large spurned pariahs in German society until their total exclusion and extermination by the Nazis in the twentieth century. Small wonder that a brilliant and ambitious woman of Rahel's ilk, who communed with the German intellectual elite of her day without ever being fully accepted by them, wanted out of her assigned role. Catalyst and quasi-saint though she may have been to others, she suffered greatly from her dual outsider status as Jew and woman.

'I wish nothing more ardently now than to change myself outwardly and inwardly,' she wrote at age 21 in a heart-wrenching letter to her friend, the German Jewish physician and thinker David Veit. 'I am sick of myself; but I can do nothing about it, and will remain the way I am, just as my face will; we can both grow older, but nothing more . . . '[24]

'Can we women folk help it if we also happen to be human?' she added, putting her position even more bluntly in another letter to Veit:

> If my mother had been kind-hearted and hard enough, and she could only have anticipated what I would become, she would have let me suffocate in the dust at my first cry. [. . .] I have such a vivid imagination; it sometimes seems to me as if an extraterrestrial being incised these words with a dagger in my heart upon

---

24 *Rahel: Ein Buch des Andenkens für ihre Freunde* (Barbara Hahn ed.), VOL. 1, pp. 23–24.

my entry into this world: 'Yes, you may be endowed with a special sensibility, you may see the world as few others see it, be great and noble, nor can I deny you a thoughtful nature. But we forgot one thing: You are doomed to be a Jewess!' And thus, my entire life is a bleeding to death! [. . .] I can trace every mishap, every calamity in life, every chagrin back to that!

Or as she phrased it in a letter to her younger sister Rose (1781–1853):

I am a Jewess, not beautiful, ignorant, without grace, without talents and instruction. Oh, my sister, it's all over; it's finished before the real finale. I could not have done anything differently. [. . .] Meanwhile, we grow old and life falls away like old dreams.[25]

Paradoxically, this very ambivalence to herself and her Jewish heritage and to her female gender role fuelled a fierce sense of self-affirmation and self-preservation:

I shall never be convinced that I am a Schlemiel and a Jewess; since in all these years and after so much thinking about it, it has not dawned upon me, I shall never really grasp it. That is why 'the clang of the murderous axe does not nibble at my root'; that is why I am still living.[26]

---

25 From a letter dated 22 May 1817; *Rahel: Ein Buch des Andenkens für ihre Freunde* (Barbara Hahn ed.), VOL. 3, p. 478.

26 From a letter to David Veit, dated 2 April 1793; *Rahel: Ein Buch des Andenkens für ihre Freunde* (Barbara Hahn ed.), VOL. 1, p. 24.

Perceiving clearly the bind the Jews were in, Rahel's pronounced ambivalence to her roots did not, however, preclude a sympathy for and identification with her people. As she put it in a journal entry dated 2 May 1823: 'People say that Jews are funny; and people often laugh at them. This comes [. . .] from their terrible situation in the contemporary European world, to be contrasted with their ancient image.'

In the wake of the so-called Hep-Hep Riots—a wave of persecution and violent attacks against Jews that broke out in various German cities in 1819, following Napoleon's ultimate defeat—Rahel wrote with an astounding perspicacity and a poignant poetic irony to her beloved brother Ludwig:

> I am abysmally sad; and in a way that I have never been. On account of the Jews. What is this host of eternal exiles to do? They, the Christians, want to keep them around; but just to torment and despise; to vilify them for their Jewish wangling; to restrict them to meagre, miserable haggling for a living; to retain them to be trodden on, and kicked down stairs. Is it the common attitude to Jews as reprehensible, corrupt through and through, that so pains me, chilling my heart? Horror of horrors! I know my country. Alas. I am a deplorable Cassandra! For three years I've been saying: they will attack the Jews . . . That is how the Germans display their pluck of indignation. And why? Because they are the most law-abiding, good-hearted, freedom-loving, authority-honouring people.[27]

---

27 See 'What is this host of eternal exiles to do?' (To Ludwig Robert-Tornow) in this volume, p. 19.

But it was only on her deathbed that she took a semblance of pride in and made some degree of peace with her Jewish heritage:

> What a history!—A fugitive from Egypt and Palestine, here I am and find help, love, fostering in you people. With real rapture I think of these origins of mine and this whole nexus of destiny, through which the oldest memories of the human race stand side by side with the latest developments. [. . .] The thing, which all my life seemed to me the greatest shame, which was the misery and misfortune of my life—having been born a Jewess—this I should on no account now wish to have missed.[28]

Whereas Amos Elon challenged the veracity of Rahel's husband's account of her ultimate acceptance of her Jewish identity, an unquestionable proto-feminist stance marked her sense of womanhood. 'This is the cause of the countless frivolities we perceive and think we perceived in women,' she wrote to her younger sister Rose,

> they have . . . no room to move their own feet, are always compelled to follow suit and extend their legs where their husband is already standing or wants to stand; and with their own eyes they perceive the whole

---

28 As per the account of her last words given by her husband Karl August in his foreword to *Rahel: Ein Buch des Andenkens für ihre Freunde* (1834), published a year after her death.

world swirling around them like someone magically metamorphosed into a tree with roots dug deep in the ground; every attempt, every wish to dissolve that unnatural state of dependence is labelled a frivolity; or worse, deemed insubordinate behaviour.[29]

*

Excluded as a Jew and a woman from playing an active role in the wheeling and dealing of high society, her salon of assembled like-minded souls served as a safe haven of her own making, a utopia of sorts, in which she and her friends, noble and bourgeois, Christians and Jews, men and women, government bureaucrats and artists, actors, officers and scholars, and sceptics of every ilk, could, if but for a few hours, shed the burden of their strictly prescribed social roles and feign complete freedom. For much of her life, Rahel reinvented herself. In this sense she succeeded in bursting out of the straitjacket of assigned social identity, transcending the limitations of a stultifying Judaism crushed into submission by the prejudices of an oppressive Christian society, and the debilitating subservient role of a woman as prescribed by men, to find a fleeting happiness in the company of others.

*

---

29 See 'Seek out distractions . . . go to places where you come into contact with new objects, words and people' (To Rose Asser) in this volume, pp. 16–17; here, p. 17.

Among other qualities, Rahel had a rare gift for friendship, which she prized above all else. As she put it in a letter to her friend from childhood, Friederike Liman:

> What is friendship? It is whatever it can be; the ability to see through the facades of other personalities, and the virtue of being able to respect others and to recognize them as independent entities, as we do ourself; the good fortune to have found someone whose nature and sheer being pleases us, in their every expression, in their every action as in each failure; someone who possesses and responds positively to the quality of allowing others to develop freely and to the best of their abilities. Thus, you permit me to remain silent when it would be difficult for me to speak—with tongue or pen—you permit me to whip off a short note that says only that which I wish to say at the present time, what I want from you![30]

In April 1831, the ailing, bed-ridden Rahel expressed in writing a last wish to her husband in a burst of words we have no cause to doubt: 'I just thought of a fitting epitaph. Let it read: Good people, if in future times anything good should happen to humanity, in your rejoicing I ask you to kindly think also of me.' Incised with these words, her tombstone in the Dreifaltigkeits (Holy Trinity) Cemetery in Berlin calls out in friendship to all passers-by with a hopeful nod at the future.

Peter Wortsman

---

30 See 'What is friendship?' (To Friederike Liman in Berlin, 4 February 1815) in this volume, pp. 73–76; here, p. 73.

TRANSLATOR'S ACKNOWLEDGEMENTS

Warm thanks to Barbara Hahn, scholar extraordinaire, for a lifetime of research on Rahel, and for her generosity in sharing her knowledge and her insights. I am especially grateful to Tess Lewis, dear friend and fellow translator, for steering me in the direction of Seagull Books, an oasis of the spirit; to its founder Naveen Kishore for graciously welcoming words from halfway around the world; and to the editorial acumen of Diven Nagpal for helping me to hone my translation into a book worthy of such a welcome.

Rahel Antonie Friederike Varnhagen von Ense, née Rahel Levin, who later assumed the family name Robert, was born in Berlin, on the first day of Pentecost, 19 May 1771. She died there on 7 March 1833, not yet 62 years old, and in the nineteenth year of our deepest and firmest loving bond of wedded bliss.

Our friends know all too well what a precious treasure and rich comfort I lost with the death of my dearly beloved wife; I need not here write of my grief; your own emotional response to her passing suffered in manifold gradations and to varying degrees will give you an inkling of how I feel. And even if the complete value of this profound soul, a woman infused with intellect and love, was not immediately apparent to all, any person who experienced but for a few moments her life force with her kindness and her passion for truth, came away with a rare and prescient impression of her most extraordinary strength of character and grace, allowing everyone to join in our lamentation.

These pages are excerpted from a lengthy foreword to *Rahel: Ein Buch des Andenkens für ihre Freunde* [Rahel: A book of remembrances for her friends], the first edition of Rahel's letters assembled in 1833 by her husband Karl August, published in Berlin in 1834, a year after her death.

Far-flung, faithful friends and trusted acquaintances have
gone to great lengths, urgently calling upon me to furnish
them with details about the last days of their beloved friend,
and friends near and far have also expressed the ardent desire
that I might, in addition, gather and provide them with a
selection of noteworthy written testimonies to her manner of
thought and extraordinary disposition, letters and such,
mementos of the deceased, affirming why she was so important and precious to so many.

My own heart impels me to fulfil both wishes, even though
I sense in advance that I am hardly up to the task. To establish
a fitting memorial to the lapsing of one of my life's greatest
joys requires a different temperament and abilities other than
those with which I have been endowed.

I will, however, gladly attempt, insofar as the present
moment permits, to accede to the friendly request. It will still
be a rich offering, however meagre it may seem to me com-
pared to what could be said. I will provide a representative
sampling from the letters, journals, memoranda and notations
of all sorts written by Rahel that I possess, which although
they cannot paint a complete picture of the person, nevertheless offer a fair approximation. From this selection, the
reader will at least be able to gauge the profound impression
that only a publication of her collected papers in their entirety,
hopefully available in the not-too-distant future, will be
able to offer.[1] At least as many of the letters as I possess, and

---

1 Karl August's initial selection of Rahel's letters was subsequently
expanded to a six-volume edition annotated and edited by Barbara

perhaps more still, are scattered all over creation, the totality of which I would like to collect, or at least assure their meticulous safekeeping!

I will not be able to confirm the selection of letters with friends beforehand. And still, this note is directed solely at friends. Unknown persons or strangers who may happen upon this text should consider the contents like that of a found letter not written to them, but for that very reason, to be read in a seemly and humble manner. I have not knowingly selected any page that might be deemed offensive to any living persons; it goes without saying that not every admonishment should be taken as such. It is not for that reason that all the names of those persons left unmentioned necessarily refer to living or very well-known individuals; conjecturing as to the identities of those unnamed persons might sometimes be difficult for the opposite reason; often enough, the reluctance to give the name has nothing to do with disguising identities. In all matters relating to Rahel, I felt compelled to take her own propensity for truth and candour as a guiding principle; she never made a secret of her life, and under no circumstances wanted her opinions and sensibilities to appear in any way different from how they really were; and the fact is, she can only win over the hearts of all noble and unbiased souls the more completely they recognize her innermost self as a fruitful ground for the

---

Hahn and published under the same name: *Rahel: Ein Buch des Andenkens für ihre Freunde* (Göttingen: Wallstein Verlag, 2011).

encounters and endeavours that enrich a life. The incompleteness of these declarations may well be the only factor that, for the moment at least, might still lead one to consider withholding certain of these communications, if, in the hearts and minds of those here considered not only as sympathetic but also as trusted readers, there be not the slightest doubt as to verity of what they read.

I have opted to precede the requested account of the last days and the passing of my beloved Rahel with a few pages recounting in brief my first encounter and acquaintance with her; these pages are part of a series of recollections from my own life, and have been lying around, already written for some time, not a word of which my dearest friend, with whom it was my compulsion and custom to communicate everything, ever read. I hope with these pages too to merit the gratitude of friends, much as such texts constitute but a feeble attempt to evoke the vivid impression of a vibrant person no words can describe. [. . .]

*

Here, too, is my recollection of a first impression. One evening, as I was reading aloud from a text by Wieland to a group of friends gathered for tea, a guest was announced, and the mention of her name elicited the kind of lively stir associated with the expectation of the uncommon and the propitious. It was Rahel Levin—or Robert, since she already went by that name at the time. I had often already heard her mentioned by various people, and always with such a special excitement in the description that I imagined the most extraordinary character, like no one else. What Count Lippe and Frau von Boye, in particular, said to me about her conjured up an energetic conjoining of intellect and human nature in its most original, purest force and form. Even when a reproach was directed at her, I, quite the contrary, divined from it the greatest praise. Much had been made of her prevailing passion, which, according to what people said of her, surpassed in greatness and exaltation and sorrow all that is said of poets. I waited with keen anticipation as smiles broke out at the impending arrival of said person.

There before me stood a slight, graceful figure, small in stature, yet powerful of build, with delicate but firm limbs, strikingly small feet and hands; her face, ringed by a halo of thick, black hair, she exuded the air of an intellectual heavyweight; her quick, albeit piercing, dark looks led one to wonder if her eyes emitted more or took more in; an expression of suffering accorded her clear facial features a gentle charm. She flitted about in her dark clothes almost like a shadow, but freely and with confidence, and her warm greeting was as easygoing as it was amicable. But what struck me as the most surprising thing about her was her sonorous, soft voice that seemed to emanate from the depths of her soul, and the most wondrous elocution that I have ever experienced. Her light, unassuming statements of the most extraordinary cast of mind and spirit combined naivety and wit, acuity and charm, and every word was imbued with a profound truthfulness, as if cast in iron, so that the most self-assured interlocutor immediately felt hard-pressed to counter or question any of her utterances. On the other hand, a benev-olent warmth of human kindness and concern allowed the least brilliant to take pleasure in her company. But all of this only came to the fore in fleeting impressions, as if in evanescent sunbursts; on this occasion there was not time enough for a complete unfolding of her depth of character. A teasing bit of badinage with Count Lippe, whose advances she had recently rebuffed, and so he wanted to get back at her, soon fizzled out, their differences resolved; the entire visit was really rather brief, and I cannot now recall any particularly quick-witted, paradoxical or otherwise striking words uttered worth citing here, but I was deeply moved by the irresistible impact of her entire being, and remained so taken by the impression she made that in the immediate wake of that remarkable encounter all I could talk and think about was her. Others made light of her aura, and since the jesting became almost annoying to me, I countered it all the more fervently by writing a poem in which I attempted to capture my impres-sion, and which, the very next day, precisely because others doubted my sincerity, I made so bold as to put in the mail, without following up or asking after her.

It would be years before I was destined to see Rahel Levin again. But her name remained an undiminished augur of magic in my soul, even though I had no inkling at the time that with that first encounter and those pert lines of verse the first link of an attachment would be forged between us, to which many more would henceforth be added, to form the most powerful turning point and the most enduring bond in my life.

Karl August Varnhagen von Ense

I

LETTERS TO FAMILY

Rahel's relations with her family, as reflected in her extensive correspondence with various family members, were at the same time intimate and intense, friendly and fraught. Upon her father's passing in 1790, after which, as a single woman, she inherited nothing, Rahel remained financially dependent on her mother's goodwill and the generosity of her older brother Markus Theodor Robert-Tornow, born Mordechai Levin (1772–1826), who took on the reins of the family business, and with whom she continued to live, albeit under sometimes strained conditions, until the time of her marriage in 1814 with Karl August Varnhagen von Ense. Her family continued to stir in her strong emotions of love, frustration and fury until her dying day.

By my reckoning, you owe me a reply

(To Markus Theodor Robert-Tornow in Breslau)

Berlin, 20 October 1787

Dear Markus,

By my reckoning, you owe me a reply; and I would not have written you if I didn't have something I wanted to request, ask and implore. On Thursday, Papa and Mama arrived here. (As I write this, I am just now being handed your letter. —I ask you again, think of us and bear in mind the consequences; just be a bit more attentive!) I immediately handed Mama a letter from Breslau received in Tuesday's mail; the letter recounts something of what we've been up to, followed by a complaint about you (just what it was the letter did not specify) and the request to admonish you; or else said letter writer would feel compelled to report to Papa. You can well imagine what effect it had on our concerned mother. Force yourself to read on, I beg you for God's sake, just for a little while longer; should I add that everyone must force

---

This missive is thought to be Rahel's earliest preserved letter, written when she was 16 years old.

themselves to do certain things, and to be moral and sensible, as you yourself have told me countless times? It's an imperative you yourself feel, as I know you all too well, even though you mask your emotions from the world. You have a level head, and a good heart too, so what else could me missing? Our situation must simply no longer be vivid and pressing enough for you to pay us any mind; just think, if Papa is burdened with complaints, Mama must bear the brunt of it. [. . .] Our mother is weak, she has suffered a great deal, and still has much to suffer [. . .] —Don't let yourself be frightened by my letter, you know that I'm somewhat prone to fear. [. . .] I beg you to employ a little reason.

With what words shall I tell what
I would rather relate to you with a single scream!

(To Markus Theodor and the Robert-Tornow family in Berlin)

Breslau, 8 August 1794

With what words shall I tell what I would much rather relate to you with a single scream! Your letter which I received this morning, and to which I hasten to reply, offers me the first sweet respite, now at 8 a.m., and to which I herewith hasten to reply. —For four days I've trundled along over deserts, fields and sand, only to find myself plunked down beside these chimneys in this damp courtyard, finally able to write you; I, who always speak to you in person! But *nobody* ever told me it would be like that. Even the regions I passed through on my journey I found passably bearable at best, and not at all lovely, which assessment at least holds for the stretch from Berlin to Krossen.* Here I sit, and a thousand fields, forests, villages and miles of paved road lie between us, not to speak of all the grains of sand, and the warp and woof of life. Not a word came to mind along the way! In short, I took a trip the like of which, as I already informed Mama, I refuse to repeat on the

---

* Krossen is a village in Brandenburg. They are on their way to Breslau.

5

way back! A chicken, a poor little chicken is, after all, a minuscule thing that gobbles up the grain strewn before it in great haste, but by God, it couldn't manage to peck at so much as a kernel of grain while waiting for that wretched travel companion of mine, Haltern, to keep still! But I soon stopped listening! [. . .] This narcissism, this inflated sense of self-importance, for the four days spent in his company I found it totally intolerable, and will once again find it inconceivable as soon as I succeed in flushing him out of my mind! All of these old wives tales, insufferably egged on by Mama, stories of old, uninteresting people, stories I already know, infused with this awful trivial morality—'the punishment befits the vice, I tell you'—this one, for example—this nonstop chatter, this being seated so close together, this espoused surprise that he should need so few handkerchiefs despite all the snuff he consumes, these vulgarities, this pawing of every foodstuff that I couldn't manage to tear out of his hands quickly enough, except for at the inns, where I could take pleasure in my own dishes, this revulsion, this everlasting talk about himself, and how he does this and that, and his ailments, and his sneezing into my hands, and his never falling asleep! Nor was I able to dwell on my own reflections; since I sat on my feet as soon as we exited the city gate (and in the city too), and almost always with my head turned to the window, but this he could not bear, since as soon as he started talking (remember what it was like to suffer his accounts), he said: 'Listen up, will you please listen!' and even grabbed hold of me!—so I was forced to look at him, just so as not to have to hear and suffer his confounded cajoling. But yesterday I closed my eyes, and so, you see, I slept through the day. Still, I was pleased to block him out! Pleased also at the absolute certainty that I would never have to suffer any convulsions; it was physically impossible. Pity me! Pity me! You who so hate pity. I don't mean, pity me, I mean, admire me for my ability to make the best of things!!! Everything happens to me. No sooner do I step out of the bath, weak-willed as I am, the next thing you know I'm off on a trip like this; I happen upon a newly established temple, a new carriage station; the stable is located directly below where we're staying; there's a wild horse attached to a chain that stamps around all night long, as if it wanted to tear down the entire house. [. . .] I'm doing all this to please Mama. I fell ill before we got to Freienwalde,* and this trip is supposed to cure me! I've always been such a schlemiel,† always giving in, since way back when; so here I am travelling with Haltern, a man with whom no one can bear to travel, and then Mama also drags along poor little Rose against her will; which makes us a party of four; but that's not all. [. . .]

Now comes the best part! Our aunt wants to travel with us to the mountains and Grüneberg—

In an open garden in Paris, I spoke with Privy Councillor Levaux, just back from Vienna, who gave a wondrous account of Frau von Arnstein, her house, princes, ministers, counts, ambassadors, gardens, dining late and all that we already

---

* A town in Brandenburg.

† *Schlemiel*, a Yiddish term for sad sack, inept, blundering person.

know about Vienna. [. . .] The gentlemen retired to the billiard room, I stayed behind with the ladies, the most insufferable sort I've ever met, I was shackled to these creatures, since it was raining and there was no escape; they tried my patience all afternoon long, and I suffered an ennui I'm not likely to ever forget!—

The city of Paris can justifiably be considered very beautiful, with so many lovely streets, and so many lovely structures and homes, the whole altogether to our liking; I also find the city quite big, and it has always been unjustly maligned. Today we're driving out to one of the smallest cloisters, as they say; and I find it to be an enormous building; I want to see them all; Madame Gasparin will take me there when I get back, and in addition, she wants to arrange for me to hear music by Mozart played by the Jesuits, music he was commissioned to write for the Latin mass, the text of which Emperor Joseph had translated into German; in short, if we see nothing else here but churches and cloisters, we will have seen some of the most remarkable sites, at least for us, who know nothing about such institutions, and hardly believe in them; I have a burning desire to first see Italy's Catholic musical sites. Therefore, I am not bored here in the least; I am absolutely thrilled to see the Jesuits. Their religious services here are lovely and pleasant to behold, since they comprise eternally magnificent music, paintings, lovely buildings, splendid scents and costumes; the overall lifestyle, however, in the women's cloister is awful; for instance, the girls' rooms are open and are fitted with altogether mediocre furniture and bad beds; the lodgings of the kindly Abbess, Baroness Mutius, are no better; the sisters take care of the sick and are called Elizabethans; every religious order is different in lifestyle and regulations; these sisters are permitted to see men, I myself saw several among them; they are not allowed to go out, and their furnishings are hardly lavish; worldly splendour is anathema to their way of life. But I have only ever dreamt of such order, good cheer and tidiness the like of which I saw there today. These young women are gardeners, pharmacists, blood letters, bread bakers, in short, they do everything; I was struck by their coarse, manly hands, of which I did not find a sole exception, and even more by their manly gait and manner of singing [. . .]; many are not religious, but those who are, pray and sing only in their mind, and amuse themselves in so doing, as I noticed; when one feels merry, she kneels down and gazes at the first best religious depiction, with which the walls are covered; in short, for any visitor who remains unamused in their presence, there is nothing more amusing than the Catholic religion; the nuns are tolerant and very courteous; they (that is to say, the abbess) conveyed many good wishes to our uncle, and invited me to come again; so they must surely have known who I was. Without intending to do so, I have told you almost everything there is to tell about this form of Catholicism; I write in great haste, convinced that any moment someone will take this missive to the post office. — So here you have fleeting news from me. I'm learning a lot along the way, and still have the mountain to climb! Adieu.

R. L.

A *Jewish wedding*

(To Markus Theodor and the Robert-Tornow family in Berlin)

Breslau, 27 August [1794]

—Our uncle, who zealously seeks out everything to amuse me, and who firmly believes that one must see everything, suggested something he hadn't in 15 years, to take me along to a Jewish wedding, to which we had, in fact, all been invited, but which only we few family members attended. I went out of curiosity; to hear Yiddish and English spoken, etc.— mortified by their lavish welcome, as if they were receiving the great sultan and a cortege from his long-lost seraglio: the heat was suffocating. But I was rewarded by the sight of a beauté, a splendid beauty, Gad's sister-in-law, all of 15 years old, pretty as a picture; many other comely young ladies were also present; there were ladies galore and with such lovely hands! [...]

A *letter of reckoning with Mother*

(To Chaie Levin in Berlin)

Berlin, 27 February 1809

Monday

Having levelled against me the easily refuted admonishment
that I simply don't know what I want, you will, I trust, be so
kind as to permit me to present my situation one last time!
You know my age; but my heartfelt distress will forever
remain a mystery to you. I am financially dependent on you:
you alone could protect me and through your loving treat-
ment grant me a sanctuary for my injured heart. This is how
things stand for me now. My sole income is what you can and
choose to grant me. No one can compute just how much a
certain sum might be worth to someone else. With a principle
of 500 Thalers in cash one can with luck or savvy become a
millionaire. But until I get married, I cannot do so. Very well
then, so be it! If my life cost more than the annuity on the sum
that I would have received as a married woman, I counter that
the same can be said for others, and that my money would
have been worth more to me. The profound respect in which
I hold your person notwithstanding, I cannot very well thank
you for granting me my freedom; had I not had it, I would

have been incensed. And you, for your part, can surely not maintain that I misused the free license I granted myself to anyone else's disadvantage; if not perhaps to my own: every individual is master over himself. Allow me to offer you an example! Which of your two daughters was until now most helpful to the family, took the greatest pains to be of service, which daughter was called upon to offer advice in times of need, which one offered succour to everyone else; and which one succeeded through her intercession in making life pleasant for all your children, your married, prized and praised daughter, or yours truly, the unhappy one? The family suffered financial loss, confusion, war and want. I lost my friends. I sought to steer clear of furtive grief, I took pains not to leave like an errant child, and so waited for the right moment, for peace, and for some clarity in your business dealings. This did not come. You moved out—to lay it on the line, like Oppenheim and company—before I had the means to get away. I was the only one adversely affected by the insolvency of the family's affairs: the Zadig ladies, the Oppenheims and my sister-in-law, Frau Levin, are all still sitting pretty. I was the one, despite my poor health, which you lump together with my needs and wants, going so far as to ask me to return a sugar bowl; I had to tap my reserves and tighten my belt at the family's losses; while others not bequeathed a dowry or inheritance still possess their silver and jewels; but of them you say: 'the poor dears!' I had nothing left except for our lodgings. I write this to elicit sympathy; but you have forgotten what sympathy is. That is what your unhappy child hopes hereby to instil in you. The summer I just lived through cannot make up for happiness. I came rushing to you thereafter in despair; upon my return I found you sick; I too was ill. Six days later you came to see me [10 October 1808], and knowing full well the extent of my malaise, my grief and fury, you came to my room, where it was dark and I lay feverish in bed, and remarked: 'Looks to me like you live in a palace! Why do you need all these rooms?' Whereupon you turned to Line: 'And your mistress is not satisfied with the food? Will you get a load of that, I send her enough to feed three!' I wept behind the bed curtain; you didn't notice; my fever doubled and brought on a migraine. I'm still crying now as I write this! I cried all day yesterday—today is Monday, a day following Moritz's arrival—and when you finally fathomed the pain that burst forth from my breast, your softened heart offered me what I most abhorred, a room overlooking Kälbermarkt. And when I requested a bedspread for my servant, you chided me for not already having one in my possession. Nobody ever asked me: Do you need something, is there anything you're lacking? Quite the contrary, they questioned why, given my meagre circumstances, I should take on a servant; and no sooner did I find suitable help, they borrowed him from me. Tell me, my dear, reasonable mother, where am I to look for love in my family? I'd be glad to find it! You gave your son ample license to run your business affairs; he never talks to me about it; and in his chagrin, he complains that I don't speak with him; I will gladly take your word for it and would be pleased to learn that he harbours loving feelings for me. I can offer ample proof of the contrary. Last summer he wrote me an unfriendly and senseless letter. In my replies I always spared *you*. Moritz now does the same with me. Previously, he and I always thought much the same of our family affairs. Insofar as possible I looked after him; he turned to me for help with every annoyance, every chagrin; ever faithful, I offered advice and did what I could. Now that I'm gone, I bid him to come to my assistance, and describe my misery in vivid terms, exactly as it is; but now all of a sudden, he treats me like a batty stranger, and does not deign to reply! Even so, I took the lead and informed him that I would be in Hamburg at the end of the month; whereupon he hastened here, but wrote to me in advance a foolish and insulting letter that I will gladly show you. So much for my dear brother's apparent eagerness to have me reside in the same city as him! When in my despair I hastened to Leipzig, hoping in my heart's mad delusion to find solace from him, he had the effrontery to inform me that he did not know when he might attend a concert with me, since his assets would lose value. At the same time, he was so foolish as to tell me—I can't recall if it was before or afterwards—that attending the last fair with a Jewish woman from Dessau cost him 400 Thalers; and when I inquired in stunned amazement how it was possible that it would cost him such an exorbitant amount, he informed me that five other girls and their fathers or relatives also came along, and since the latter never spoke of paying, the bill amounted to the aforementioned sum. In this regard he is, of course, quite right: whoever works can spend his resources as he sees fit; and I am glad to benefit from my share; but must he treat me with such insolence and foolishness! In short, I am obliged to suffer indignities from all sides, without any regard for the effect on me of what they all take for granted. Ludwig Robert, the gracious one, as you well know, is the sole exception: he knows that I love him; and you know that that is all. Much as you might wish it, Mother dearest, you cannot in good faith recommend this bunch then as my friends; in a conversation of a mere 15 minutes, I could cite many other examples of familial discord.

I had already gotten so much off my chest that I appealed to Campan for money. This foreign-born gentleman whom I only frequented for a year, and who was not my lover, instilled in me the courage to dare ask. Why? Because he loves and respects me. I no longer harbour any delusions: my brothers are my brothers by birth; and they will always be that. But they have yet to prove themselves to be my friends by their conduct, rather than by any single action. In all of life's trials and tribulations they always found me to be loving, as I am to all who approach me. To this very day I have always kept my heartache a secret, even if I was not always adroit at hiding the truth; this I know to be true; and will make no more effort to mask the truth. Nor should you for any reason advise me to do so. But permit me, now and in the future, as long as I remain unwed, to be financially dependent on you; that is the only entreaty that I dare make of you! As these will be the last words you will hear from me about my abject state of affairs.

Rahel

Seek out distractions . . . go to places where you
come into contact with new objects, words and people

(To Rose Asser in Brussels)

Karlsruhe, Friday, 22 January1819, Noon. Warm rainy weather.

[. . .] Seek out distractions [. . .] go to places where you come into contact with new objects, words and people . . . We women are doubly in need of this; whereas the activities of men involve business transactions that they at least find significant, the exercise of which flatters their ambitions, activities in which their perceived professional advancement flatters their sense of self [. . .]; we women only engage piecemeal in small tasks and household contingencies that drag us down, forever following the lead of men. It is an aberrant distortion, a consequence of anthro-ignorance,* when people persuade themselves that our female spirit is different from that of men and geared to other wants and needs than theirs, and that, for example, we might be inclined to live off the existence of a husband or a son. This presumption is solely based on the premise that in her heart of hearts, a woman aspires to nothing more than to accede to the demands and needs of her husband

---

* *Menschenunkunde*, roughly human ignorance, a term coined by Rahel.

in this world, or the wishes of her children; in that case, every marriage would as such be the highest human condition; but that is not the case; and we love, nurture, cultivate the wishes of our nearest and dearest; acquiesce to their demands; make that our key concern and most pressing preoccupation; such selfless commitment cannot, however, fulfil, revive and bestir us to self-sustaining actions; nor can it fortify and reinforce our purpose in life. This is the cause of the countless frivolities we perceive and think we perceived in women: they have . . . no room to move their own feet, are always compelled to follow suit and extend their legs where their husband is already standing or wants to stand; and with their own eyes they perceive the whole world swirling around them like someone magically metamorphosed into a tree with roots dug deep in the ground; every attempt, every wish to dissolve that unnatural state of dependence is labelled a frivolity; or worse, deemed insubordinate behaviour. [. . .]

Consulting Dr Teufel

(To Ludwig Robert-Tornow)

Friday, 19 March 1819

We are once again enjoying better, more temperate summer weather. But I am stuck in a miserable mood that I can't seem to kick. I'm not a god; in my house too many other unstoppable, incalculable, would-be deities already lord it over me, darkening my mood at every moment of the day; I find them very trying, and feel truly done in. Let this inky outcry suffice! It will also explain why I haven't written you. On Friday, on account of my multiple complaints, I had them call Dr Teufel.*

---

* It is not clear if the name of the physician in question really was Dr Teufel, of if Rahel so dubbed him. In German, *der Teufel* is the Devil.

What is this host of eternal exiles to do?

(To Ludwig Robert-Tornow)

August 1819

I am abysmally sad; and in a way that I have never been. On account of the Jews. What is this host of eternal exiles to do? They, the Christians, want to keep them around; but just to torment and despise; to vilify them for their Jewish wangling; to restrict them to meagre, miserable haggling for a living; to retain them to be trodden on, and kicked down stairs. Is it the common attitude towards Jews as reprehensible, corrupt through and through, that so pains me, chilling my heart? Horror of horrors! I know my country. Alas. I am a deplorable Cassandra! For three years I've been saying: they will attack the Jews . . . That is how the Germans display their pluck of indignation. And why? Because they are the most law-abiding, good-hearted, freedom-loving, authority-honouring people.

Written in the wake of the Hep-Hep Riots of 1819.

Half an artist

(To Ludwig Robert-Tornow in Karlsruhe)

Friday, 10 a.m., 27 October 1826
Springlike weather with a little morning dew.

Gillyflower, pansy, everything grows outdoors; the most luscious looking bunches of grapes heaped in barrels are arrayed on the steps of fruit stands, the earth green as in summer, trees again in bloom; but for the last five, six days the leaves have begun to fall; for the last two hours the wind hasn't kept blowing from the same direction; there's a blast of cold air from the south; people who were sick have a hard time recovering, myself at the head of the list. Fists and thumb joints on both hands swollen with gout. Extremely irritated nerves. Let this serve as an excuse for me and my writing, and what I don't write, and for my wretched handwriting.

The day before yesterday, my precious, dear friend, I wanted to write to you, just when your letter arrived, since that very day I saw the exhibition again—for the third time; the first time I got very sick, spent eight days in bed, three weeks at home; the second time I had a bad flareup; and now, the third time, I suffered a mildly unpleasant relapse, but on the advice of my physicians, common sense and diet have since restored me to good health—I went expressly to see Rike's painting,* everyone is talking about it, each in their own way; hear what I have to say. It is in many respects a well-made, desirable painting. A painter able to paint such a perfect likeness of a lovely person tears his own laurel branches from the tree out of which we must weave a wreath. Eyes, forehead, hair, superbly depicted; stance, countenance! Enough said. Whosoever can capture the expression of such perfect features is half an artist; whoever can reproduce them is a complete artist.

---

* Rike is the diminutive of Friederike, the first name of Rahel's brother Ludwig Robert-Tornow's wife.

Strain your wit to write to me, but spare your purse

(To Friederike Robert-Tornow in Berlin)

Friday, 15 May 1829

Dear Rika! I am writing herewith to expressly forbid you to give me a gift on the first day of Pentecost!!! Strain your wit to write to me, but spare your purse. I give you my word of honour that, aside from a fresh-cut flower carried in person to my door, I will accept nothing. You can ask Ludwig if such words are uttered in vain. I wanted to celebrate my holiday in my own way, with a gathering in Bartholdy's garden, pining after summery weather, and with much more bodily strength than I will be able to muster all summer long. I had hoped to host an outdoor breakfast there, and to hold court. But such festivities are not for me in my current state; and I will surely pout all day if I'm up to it. It just occurred to me that you could very well write me a poem. For heaven's sake, please don't buy me the half dozen napkins—that, too, occurred to me—you'll soon be receiving the same from me. I implore Ludwig to send me that blasted poem about that scoundrel Platen, fallen into disrepute and henceforth persona non grata at my gatherings. Ludwig no doubt made light of the link between the poet's name Platen and *platt* [i.e. platitudinous].

II

LETTERS TO DAVID VEIT

A nephew by marriage of Rahel's childhood friend Brendel
Mendelssohn-Veit (aka Dorothea Schlegel), David Veit (1771–1814),
a cultivated young Jewish medical student of intellectual bent and
boundless curiosity, initiated a lively and extensive correspondence
with the young Rahel Levin that would soon be conceived by both
as a serious intellectual colloquy, a reckoning by two young people,
both of whom struggled with their Jewish identity in a largely hostile
Christian culture. Veit later moved to Hamburg, where he became a
respected physician. He died of an infection contracted while caring
for a patient in 1814.

My incorrect writing

Berlin, 18 November 1793

—So let me tell you exactly what I know about my incorrect writing, without wanting to sound the least bit apologetic, since I do not feel myself at all attacked by your question. Much as I resolve to pay heed to orthography while reading, I almost never manage, and if I do so at the very start of reading something, I don't really read, but just see the way the words are written; I soon grow tired of it and return to reading; this makes me feel terribly sad for myself, and the simplest soul can learn more than me, and it would be insufferable if I did not find some small consolation in not blaming the faulty side of my mind, but rather acknowledging that it is the good side that ill serves me. It is true that I always think of the essential import of what I'm reading, and that to do so I apply all the means at my disposal, and promptly forget all about it; I arrange in my mind the aggregate of all that I hear and read, and if, as often occurs, I am reminded of irrelevant things, I quickly put them back where they belong, and keep grappling with the problems at hand, but without ever dwelling on the intellectual process of how I go about it.

Consequently I learn nothing, and so am ill-equipped to teach anyone anything; all who give me instruction begin by preaching from a vantage point alien to my way of thinking, speaking for hours on end without any connection that I am able to grasp; even though I prick up my ears with the greatest concentration, since among other matters, they allude to things that I would have long since liked to know, and which I could use in my limited store of knowledge; that's how matters have always gone for me with all masters, and so I only fathom now long after the fact the little I remember of what they told me, since I never grasp the meaning of answers to questions I did not myself pose, and such masters spew dozens of answers one after another, and how in heaven's name can a person take it all in! —How deeply gratifying that you are now so diligent in your studies, knowledge is the only power you can procure for yourself if you don't already have it, power is strength, and strength is everything. If, when push comes to shove, we find that all of our speculations amounted to nothing but smoke and mirrors, it is the truly useful knowledge that puts us ahead of, or behind others, as the case may be; knowledge that in and of itself affords great satisfaction. But how, pray tell, come Easter, will I be able to establish that you have really learnt something, other than that you say so and I believe you? I won't be able to judge for myself, save through the inference of somebody else; if you keep writing to me 'I learn something new every day', then I will know that many days will have passed and much knowledge will have been acquired by Easter. I beg you, dear Veit, write these words often to me; and do keep up the good work, don't let yourself be distracted, as I am here, even upon fathoming that people find you amusing. [. . .] Don't permit yourself to be peeved, and don't bother to consider all the discouraging things people might say or give you to understand, etc.; don't dwell either on the foolishness or the wisdom they may find in you; and another thing I beg you: for God's sake, avoid putting anything off for later. Just think that if the ordinary present moment is a goddess, then the time spent at a collegium or some other academic endeavour, or the time you spend in Göttingen is the god of gods, and that a mere spark of the benefit and influence of time so spent far surpasses time spent in any other way. It may be madness for me to try to persuade you of this, but it only sounds like that; I am in this regard the greatest ignoramus in the world who puts so much store in knowledge, and not out of frightened ignorance [. . .] Nothing in the world can help me now, and I am compelled to expend all my energy for naught, and can find solace in my communion with few other people, even if they appear to abound in knowledge; since most of the purportedly erudite folk are, in fact, stupid, rambling and pedantic! —Therefore, please do me the honour and teach me something, so that I may take pleasure in it. Dear Veit, I sense that I must also admit to a certain restive concern. You hear me bemoan and jabber so much about my ignorance and suddenly make such a big to do about intellectual expertise, and set such a damned great store in knowledge; but don't think for a moment that I have thereby forfeited the one benefit of my ignorance, a jaunty insouciance, the only endearing aspect of not knowing—at least not in the eight weeks of your absence—all of the utterances you hear me spouting here are nothing but an outburst of what has been swirling around in my head for the longest time . . .

I will be as diligent as I possibly can; as much as I can master, I will have learnt, and as to the rest, all of what I won't manage to master, I will, as in the past, graciously embrace my deficiency without envy, presumption, annoyance, or foolish wonderment. [. . .]

Yes, I waltz

Berlin, 17 December 1793

[. . .] Yes, I waltz. For the past five Mondays we've established a dance hour at home—ever since the third session I kicked up my legs and started waltzing, and not half badly; and do you think a girl can keep a steady head with all that unwholesome twisting and turning? —Though I can't quite take the sensual pleasure in it that most people do, half of them picturing it as perilous to their health, the other half as sheer heavenly delight; or do you have to be so much in love, like Werther,* to not let anyone else grab your girl, because you find it so delightful? —Based on my experience, I swear, I don't know anything quite like it, extreme muscle pain notwithstanding—(I will leave out the 'consequently') there is nothing as unconducive to thinking or to feeling as this German swinging. Still, it's a treat—namely, as never-ending occupation, because you have to keep moving not to miss a step; but your movements become so mechanical that you ultimately do stop thinking and seeing—as you spin around

---

* A reference to *The Sorrows of Young Werther*, published in 1774, a bestselling epistolary novel about a young man's intensely emotional response to unrequited love, ultimately leading to suicide, by the young Johann Wolfgang von Goethe.

the room in the ghastliest circles. Following this impartial account, you will take me for very level-headed—and you may well be right in so supposing—except that in this regard you're mistaken—*I* am one of the most avid and tireless waltzers, and have become so accomplished as to elicit my brothers' praise—and they're crass characters, as in Goethe's book. Now you're likely convinced that I've had my fill of movement? Apropos of which, no market barker employing all the tricks of the trade could possibly be more fit than me after the last fair; and don't I keep going for the hour, and oftentimes all day—despite feeling beat, you'd better believe it. You see, I don't feel the slightest bit fatigued; can you imagine, even the strain on my eyes has subsided; I can read for as long as I like the same evening—and would often do so, if I didn't consider enough sleep to be necessary to my health. Just to experience such a felicitous revolution! I, who couldn't walk any longer, and had calmly given up all hope of ever doing so again, can keep going like a child, and keep dancing for hours on end. You see, that's the real reason I dance—it's a religious service for me, a kind of thanksgiving, and perhaps also a sacrifice, since it definitely does tire me out. So, from such apparent inadvertence you wouldn't believe that this girl has firmly resolved, come summer, to take the cold cure again—and I really do plan to do so. It's because of all the dancing and all the festivities, opera rehearsals, concerts and visitors dropping by these days that I haven't written for such a long time, and that's why I am now writing in such a disconnected, disjointed and multifarious manner . . .

Learning to lie

Berlin, 18 February 1794

Afternoon

I trust I can tell you something that happened the other day? [. . .] Last Monday at table, Markus conducted an interrogation, grilling the children, after discovering a naughty bit of mischief: the name Levin scrawled on the wall in the hallway near my room. Little Rosa declared with a giggle: 'It wasn't me!'; Ludwig likewise insisted: 'Me neither!'; only Moritz lied, insisting: 'I don't even have a pencil!' sticking with his denial; frightened with good reason, he gave the same answer 16 or 17 times to every question with which he was peppered in cross-examination, as if at a real interrogation; the colour of his face was a dead giveaway, but he even tried to quell the reddening, and kept repeating: 'But I don't even have a pencil!' He finally more or less conceded his guilt, and even though the entire business smacked of a foolish prank, they wanted to intimidate him into making a complete confession; so, I said: 'He can't very well admit it; isn't it enough that he denied it!' Well pleased with my words, no sooner uttered than I burst out laughing. The thought came to me in a flash before formulating it in words. So be it! It was the sound of the words in my ears that unleashed laughter. But that wasn't the end of it, when at long last Moritz confessed, Mama said: 'Best not to lie, but rather to admit, I did it, but didn't know it was naughty, and I won't do it again.' Whereupon, the boy responded forthrightly: 'I first wanted to see if I could get away with it.' It was a fabulous fib; you really should have been there and seen his face. I thought it over; I tried my best to moderate the interrogation, and after I took pains to drape the tell-tale writing on the wall with a thick cloth, they went so far as to tear it down; all this untruth didn't sit well with me, seeing as the boy (being a child) didn't have a clear idea of the fault of what he'd done, and much as he tried to save face, he was terrified anew by the awful crime with which he was confronted; and this residual fear and chagrin always has an insidious effect on a child's character, which is why I found it so distressing to witness; I took great pains, presuming general approval, to transform this ill-conceived interrogation as much as possible into an exercise in persuasion, but found myself all the more misunderstood, and the whole business continued a while; though I believe that Markus sensed what I was trying to do. —Why should children be expressly forbidden from fibbing and fabricating excuses? These are talents that (alas!) one needs to learn; children are brought up to face life's harsh realities, not to live in some idealized heaven in which a pure heart and a clear conscience are lauded. More tomorrow. Adieu, I've got to pay somebody a visit.

Evening, after 10 p.m.

Back to the business about the children. Why not teach them
that lies, lying and weaselling excuses are a necessary evil, and
thereby demonstrate to them the harsh reality, just as with
other hard work that we stop doing of our own free will when
no longer called for, to spare our hands—this as a way to
nurture conscience! Infernal morality, could cultivated inquisi-
tion not lead to the slow roasting of my already precarious
renommé? And that would not even be the worst of it; such
inquisitorial morality also smacks of foolishness or stupidity,
since it seems infeasible; in the truest sense of the word I feel
this as well as someone who hears it; but one can make
children understand without preaching, and preach to them
ad nauseam without bringing the message home, and that
there can be no effective preaching without clearly introducing
the relevant issues through our actions at the right time and
place; that's what I believe, until you or someone else can con-
clusively prove the contrary! Bonsoir! [. . .]

My entire life is a slow bleeding to death

22 March 1795

[. . .] I have such an imagination; as if when I was driven into this world, an otherworldly being had, upon my entry, carved these words with a dagger into my heart: 'Yes, do have a special sensibility, see the world as few others see it, be great and noble, nor can I deprive you of a constant reflection on the way things are. But one thing has been forgotten: Be a Jewess, a Jewish woman!' And therewith, my entire life is a slow bleeding to death; holding me in check, it delineates my miserable existence; every movement, every effort to subdue the curse is a new death; and motionlessness will only be possible in death . . . I can trace every affliction, every misery, every chagrin back to that [. . .]

If only I could open myself to people
the way one opens a cabinet

Berlin, 1 June 1795

[. . .] —Why would you not want to show anyone else a letter of mine from beginning to end? I wouldn't mind it one bit, nothing is off limits to be seen. Do you not want the truths I sometimes tell or the openness we have with each other to be seen? I don't understand why not. If only I could open myself up to people the way one opens a cabinet, and with a single gesture reveal everything arranged in an orderly fashion on shelves. They would surely be pleased, and as soon as they see it, understand. [. . .]

I think I just wrote you
the most confused letter ever written

Teplitz, 28 August 1795

I think I just wrote you the most confused letter ever written: it couldn't hurt to follow with this one. How I came to dash off such a hasty missive, blame it on the lack of time; and as I was writing it, I was well aware that I really wanted to say something else, and just let my quill keep moving out of lassitude, so that you would nevertheless have word from me. I had second thoughts about what I'd written you after the fact, for all the good it did. Quite the contrary. It seems to me that a blind man must be able to read between the lines of my maintaining how very glad I am, not to be unhappy, and fathom that I could not possibly be happy. I mean a long-suffering happiness. The reason for the suffering doesn't matter. That is true happiness; and I'm afraid I have even lost the capacity. —And you spoke of the quiet kind. —For this precise reason, I cannot permit myself to be implicitly taken in by anyone, which is why I never idolize anything or anyone. [. . .]

The greatest artist, philosopher or poet
has nothing on me

Tuesday, 16 February 1805

It is impossible to write to someone with whom one would like to spend one's life. What thoughts, what gasps of relief would one not like to express, to show? He could be our witness, confirm one's existence! [. . .] I feel a great flood of tears welling up in my breast, overwhelming my heart [. . .] Nothing seems singular to me any more; I feel altogether trapped and my spirit is livelier than ever. I do not console myself with the prospect of life hereafter! A pleasant life here on earth would not preclude happiness in the hereafter. Every moment heightens my ever-more profound sense of inconceivable loss! Our organs are too finite to grasp it; and higher beings surely mourn our incapacity [. . .] The coldest, the least that we mere mortals can do—the great pain, the great loss, the impossibility of shedding the aforementioned confusion in any way other than by dying, parting, separating, being isolated, serves only to make death possible. You can take this declaration to be as all-encompassing as you like [. . .] You see, I know full well why you don't write to me! You've found a great happiness. [. . .] What lady friend have you selected, found and taken to heart! I absolutely understand what makes a person, what makes *you* tick. I have the capacity, as if constituted with a double self, to lend out my soul, and have the inordinate capacity to split myself in two without risking obfuscation. I am as singular as the greatest soul on earth. The greatest artist, philosopher or poet has nothing on me. We are made of the same stuff. We are of the same stature, and belong together. And he who seeks to exclude the other only excludes himself.

What good does it do, my friend,

to look into happiness with strange eyes?

Berlin, 20 April 1811

I thank you right heartily, dear Veit, for your congratulations. But what good does it do, my friend, to look into happiness with strange eyes, as the English poet puts it!* The mood of the words that follow will needs must be the reverse of my brother's stance; and so, a burst of reflections will converge, even if they don't necessarily follow one from another. (I cannot go on writing now, since, as soon as I pick up my pen, only the most profound musings of heart and soul escape from my lips, and nothing else comes to mind. But these musings are mostly critical, or lyrical; and neither, it seems, is suitable to me; to what I, as a woman, d'un certain age, and still a mademoiselle, am, and what I am supposed to be. It is from

---

This is an excerpt from Rahel's last letter to Veit prior to his death from an infection contracted while tending to patients.

* William Shakespeare, *As You Like It* 5.2.45–46: 'O, how bitter a thing it is to look into happiness through another man's eyes!'

this perspective that I bid you to consider the explanations—les déclarations—that will comprise this letter.) Rest assured that I regret nothing that I have done, and most especially that I have refrained from doing; that I still think much the same as I have always thought, and if a conceptual difference is to be found between my mindset in the past and now, you must know that it is only a modification, a further development and substantiation of my own nature; that is, more comprehensive, clearer, more coherent rationales for my positions, and a sharpening of all my inclinations and aversions. I remain untutored, self-taught, as I have always been, 'but grasp what wise men say'; and the history of matters with which thinkers of all kinds and erudite folks concern themselves is also my history and the object of my preoccupations. Such thoughts arise as a function of my nature, and despite—not because of—my environment; consequently, they feed my soul and make me happy. Now I will be able to tell you clearly in a few words how things stand for me. It may well be ten years ago that I said to you: 'Rest assured that nothing will change for the worse so long as I still live in my garret room, and have Line to look after me.' Unfortunate circumstances drove me from my garret room a year and a half ago. Line is still with me. [. . .] I am profoundly superstitious, a fact to which I confess in complete sincerity. [. . .] I have suffered great illnesses. All of my strengths and functions are in a muddle. [. . .] And it is no joke when I say that my body—

the composite of body and soul*—asks of my spirit† and heart if they want to go on living. I haven't seen my doctor for an entire year. Last summer he offered poor medical care, despite which I got better; so, it seems, I was to go on living: I had sufficient reserves of strength! Now you know all that can be said about me in words. Please write back, so that I can hear the same about you! And be assured that not even you can turn me against you.

Rahel

---

* Rahel coins a word *Körperseele*, presumably a composite of body and soul.

† Rahel uses the German word *Geist*, which encompasses spirit, mind and intellect, for which there is no adequate one-word English translation.

III

LETTERS TO VARIOUS FRIENDS

Rahel had countless friends from all walks of life, including actresses, artists, authors, high official and diplomats from various countries, some of whom she regularly frequented, and with others maintained an extensive correspondence.

Those are the chosen ones, the wormlike ones among us

(To Karl Gustav von Brinckmann in Hamburg)

Berlin, July 1800

Dear Brinckmann! [. . .] How are you? The words waft over my lips. What's the use, you're still a silkworm, I too am a worm. We are all worms. The happy ones keep spinning. I keep spinning up a storm: and the most laudable, the most precious, the gladdest thing is that I'm still spinning away at my first thread. Those are the chosen ones, the wormlike ones among us. On Sunday, Jean Paul stopped by; I was witty—I had just spent eight very witty days, spouting all manner of curious expressions and bon mots—not him. Which was a good thing. He had something downright calming about him. His manner did not make me feel ashamed. Never did a person look so completely different from the way I had imagined him. Not a trace of the comic. He looks sharp-witted, and his forehead is bursting with thoughts. He speaks in such a serious, soft and serene, and orderly manner, is so inclined to listen—in a sweet and fatherly way, I might add—that I never would have imagined he was a Richter.*

---

* Here, Rahel toys with the German author Jean Paul's family name, Richter, which translates in English as 'judge'.

What kind of fear!

(To Georg Wilhelm Bokelmann in Bordeaux)

Paris, 20 April 1801

My dear, what kind of fear does it take! Nothing, not one of my panic attacks could prompt me to attempt to express with my pen the pain that presses down upon and torments my heart; only the conviction that you welcome seeing words from me—written words! hated, yes, hated words!—I flatter myself, that this alone could prompt me to put it into words. A profound fatigue of the sort that I have seldom experienced made my life, so to speak, stop dead in its tracks; at 11 p.m., I went to bed. Nothing, I believed, but the sleep of death could relieve and dissolve such mortal fatigue: consumed by such thoughts and feelings, I lay down to sleep; but the first few hours were all muffled by a languid state somewhere between sleep and wakefulness; only now do I remember that I did not even, as is my wont, strain to fall asleep. But I did sleep, a very deep and refreshing sleep, from which I awakened, feeling perfectly healthy, my complexion altogether pale and healthy-looking, the weather as nice as can be; but what a morning! All of which led up to a cataclysmic bout of fear. I can say no more; and can't compel myself to emit another word.

Although speaking and writing are of no help,
one ought not therefore to stop speaking and writing!

(To Regina Frohberg)

Berlin, 13 December 1801

Read this letter as if it only arrived eight days from today.

I wrote it yesterday. It's a good one.

Although speaking and writing are of no practical help, one ought not therefore to stop speaking and writing! Take this dark sentence, whereof each half is only true in and of itself, as nothing but a jest! I was not clear in what I said this morning; and you did not rightly understand me. The subject we were talking about is too important to me, we also came to a point at which things had to be made clear—all the more so, since present partial understanding needs must lead to mis-understanding, so I feel compelled to continue to the best of my ability and based on my best judgement.

What we actually understand by the word *human being* is a creature able to establish reasonable contact with its own kind, in accordance with consciousness, based on which we are able to mould ourselves and also feel impelled to keep moulding ourselves. We may be as we wish, we may do as we wish, but we feel compelled to be congenial with one another.

We all follow the self-same beautiful, pure, most human, most amiable impulse. Mankind's entire fabric of life is in the broadest sense—but also down to the most minute—nothing but this premise modified ad infinitum. But what in the world is more amicable—and happier—than a soul open to everything that matters to mankind! And what, on the other hand, produces a purer spirit than this open state of mind that elevates and propagates itself by its duration, by its mere existence! The whole world benefits from you, just as you benefit from the world! [. . .] Just imagine at any given moment that it suddenly strikes you what it means to be gracious and kind, and voilà, that's what you are! Not as you wrote to me today, that 'it is an effort that I demand of myself'—at which I am now inept, at which one is always inept—but rather, what I demand of myself is a moment of conviction, a moment of healthy belief.

More mortified than me you cannot be, more misery than mine you cannot savour; you cannot experience greater misfortune in all matters of paramount or minimal significance to yourself; you cannot see more dreams founder; you cannot have had a more anguished youth than I had until age 18; you cannot have been sicker, nor closer to the brink of madness; nor could you have loved more ardently. But when through it all did the world not speak to me, when was I not touched by everything human, when did I not take an interest in human emotions: in anguish and art and jest! At the moment when pain and nagging regret wrench the soul apart, one cannot, must not succumb to the urge to bury treasures of the spirit.

One must then draw on one's reserve of spiritual treasures, one's reserve of interest in things human, one's interest in humanity itself. Don't tell me in response that it is only one's natural gifts that enable one to do so; and, for instance, that I should not compare myself to you. Whosoever has the intellectual capacity to reason as you can about certain matters is endowed with great strengths; only his interests are misdirected.

A cultivated person is not a person on whom nature has lavished gifts; a cultivated person is, rather, one who kind-heartedly, wisely and judiciously expends the limited natural gifts he has been given, and for the greatest good; one who does so of his own free will; a person who has a clear sense of what he lacks, one who can acknowledge his failings. This is in my view a matter of duty, and not a natural knack; and by my way of thinking, it is this and this alone that constitutes a truly cultivated person. That is why I urge you to finally acknowledge with your own eyes what you neglect. What I mean is to raise your frame of reference to the universal—à généraliser—; not that the generalized leads you to the particular, but the other way around. This would make you altogether amicable. You can arrive at this realization, since it comes suddenly through a thought; just as, in your case, the contrary occurs through a thought. I also repeat what I have already said: people like us find health when they conceive the greatest revulsion for being sick; when they are thoroughly convinced that being healthy is most desirable. [. . .]

Love is so much the stuff of life

(To Regina Frohberg in Berlin)

Monday, Berlin, 29 September 1806. Noon.

Our servant Feu will bring you this note. He is a Jew, and they are forbidden to live anywhere or marry without a special dispensation: consequently, he has two children who, according to the law, are bastards; but now the mother of these children, who is also Jewish, has been expelled from Berlin. (He himself will tell you to what extent the Jewish community leaders are themselves embroiled in this affair.) Your friend, City Councillor Rück, ought to be able to help him. You can guess the rest for yourself. Let a two-fold love, ours and theirs, come to the aid of this loving couple. Love is so much the stuff of life, such that even a semblance of it elicits my best wishes, and taps my eternal concern! [. . .]

R. L.

As long as you live, you love, if you've ever loved anyone

(To Regina Frohberg in Berlin)

Berlin, October 1806

Dear child,

As long as you live, you love, if you've ever loved anyone.[*]
And this suffering is one of the best. How should I help you
when I cannot even help myself! I will not balk against the
beat of my own heart; such is my art. It is no great accom-
plishment; I am not any happier than the most acquiescent,
or however else you want to put it. I cannot change myself; I
have no desire to be a martyr. I expect nothing of people; all
the less from those I love. They will not love me any the more
for it! And Goethe says: 'People don't understand each
other'—I say, we don't understand the world: and the blissful
moments must be treasured. Pretty posturing! It doesn't make
me any happier. I am alone. And reading *Hermann von
Lübeneck*,[†] I share your opinion, but I'm just at the beginning.

---

[*] Froberg's second published novel, *Schmerz der Liebe* (The pain of
love) is a roman à clef lampooning Berlin society, in which a fictionalized
Rahel is one of the characters.

[†] *Hermann von Lübeneck, oder Geständnisse eines Mannes* (Hermann
von Lübeneck, or confessions of a man) (1806) by I. A. Köhler.

By the way, the war bores me. The stagnation. You see, I too would like to have some fun. Call it a yen, if you like. All cruelty comes from higher spheres. My mathematics isn't worth a penny. It won't make me any richer. Adieu. Be of good cheer. I am! And soon will be. Stop taking the medicine.

The storm is raging so fiercely on my rooftop
that the eaves are trembling

(To Regina Frohberg in Berlin)

Sunday, 28 December 1806

Last night, I was so tired I could well have slept like a log; but believe me, the storm is raging so fiercely on my rooftop that the eaves are trembling, as if a carriage were rolling over them. I often took fright—I fear that our house, and, in particular, our roof may not withstand the force; and despite the childish fatigue, I would have taken refuge downstairs; but the others would have pestered me all morning with carrying bath water. In short, sleep took hold again; and today—immediately following my bath—I don't yet feel the least bit feverish. Oh, you can't believe how jubilant I'd be if only I felt a little bit well! That's how things stand with my health: it's all all right for the moment, the few salutary means are so effective, always the same; and one might well put it this way, that it's a real blow against my body when it falls ill; then the weather, the air in my room, or some condition you find in the southern clime would have helped. +

This cross marks the spot where I was disturbed, and the disturbance is likely to last a good half hour: a person can find no peace here! A pox on them! [. . .] +

Just picture this: first Nette Markuse dropped by, which didn't affect me one way or another; and in her presence I already felt my fever rise; then came my sister-in-law with her children, Hanne and Fanny, their presence didn't much bother me either; then came her brother, Louis, who rubbed me the wrong way: his very appearance on the scene, his mere presence annoys me; it has a deleterious physical effect on my body. We only spent three minutes alone together, and you could see the consternation! For a moment he held his eyes shut; and seething with rage, I didn't say a word. What do you make of my cowardice, my baseness? Weakness is something altogether different. He just wielded the power over me to annoy me, undisturbed, by his entire being. If only I could flee this accursed Berlin: leave this place where I am who I am, and escape somewhere where nobody knows me. Everybody is getting on my nerves these days, without realizing it! I had intended to write something altogether different, and at length, before inserting the crosses as place holders; but then I became annoyed on account of all the aforementioned nonsense. You have no idea how much ire, how much bitterness, how much hatred of everything I hate and of all those I hate Louis arouses in me!!! —And how remotely, how little, and how inadequately my response reflects what I really feel!!!

This morning I remarked that when something awful happens to you, even something physical, you only complain about it once it's over.

Then yesterday evening, I remarked that, contrary to what one might suppose, people who oftentimes resort to excuses, and for whom lies are neither uncommon nor anathema, and since childhood a familiar and practicable ploy they keep up their sleeve, are the very people one can easily bamboozle in an impromptu fashion, and without any concerted effort to do so; it's really quite simple! And I have already found an explanation. Such people are forever concerned with the day's little doings—things that keep propagating their little lies— so taken up by appearances that they take little notice of or misinterpret a person's manner, voice, tone, look, countenance, stance, soul and nature; and, in particular, misconstrue sly subterfuge and contrivances for the hallmarks of true wisdom, which they seldom ascribe to others; above all doubting daydreamers, which is what they call soulful types. This is quite true. (It's afternoon now. I had to take a break from letter writing to grab a bite.)

I had already planned to write you this missive yesterday evening; but I neglected to tell you why I did not do so. And if I see you alone this evening, I'll tell it all to you in person. Don't bother trying to guess: it's just a matter of my mood. You'll find out soon enough.

Can you imagine, that among other things, Louis has taken to asking me if I am well-disposed towards him? Just to annoy me! But he won't get a word out of me. [. . .]

A *picture of pure stupidity*

(To Regina Frohberg in Berlin)

Friday, 9 January 1807

At seven o'clock in the morning, my dear Sniffles,* Humboldt will come by to pick me up; you can consequently calculate—while putting your mind at rest—the time it will take us to get there. It pains me to think that you should have fallen ill precisely while planning our mutual gratification, and oh, how dreadful to think that you should have had such a rough time of it! That, too, will pass, as you yourself say; as will the noxious effect of the medicine, as frantic as you were to get hold of it. Here's hoping that you will be well enough today to take part in the gathering and to listen to the lecture. But only if you're really feeling up to it.

Koreff's letter is the worst I've read for as far back as I can remember. Please do me the favour and hold on to it! We'll have to go through it together and analyse it from a literary standpoint, if you will. I've never read anything more flat,

---

* An untranslatable term of endearment, *Schnäuzchen* is roughly equivalent to 'Sniffles'.

empty, inexpressive and tiresome. It really is like something overblown, puffed up, with nothing in it. A picture of pure stupidity. Jule's letter, on the other hand, is a tender-hearted emanation of the most charming, big-hearted, priceless wit. A rich reserve of heartfelt humour! She offered what he, Koreff, was sorely lacking, and came up with decent, substantive counterarguments for his pointless, fruitless bombast. Completely taken aback by his letter, as she must have been— or at least I would have been—she nevertheless managed to find a charming, womanly, well-mannered, naturally witty and coherent response to his small-minded stuff and nonsense. Dear God! If only such talent and diligence were shared by others! Adieu, Becka, dearest! You can keep Koreff's letter. R. L.

On translation

(To Regina Frohberg in Berlin)

31 January 1807

With the word 'translation' I never mean anything other than to bestir, by whatever means, in the language into which a text is to be translated, the mood and the impression aroused by the original. I even consider literal translation to be impossible: since no two languages are ever alike; the most literal rendering can be found in a dictionary, and is therefore nothing but a word repository, devoid of any other significance or consequence.

Upon reading Parny's short dialogue, and finding it so well written, and also deeper than I presumed, I thought for a moment that such sentiments could only be expressed in a European tongue, and I wished, for others' sake, that it might be rendered in our language; and the inkling of a thought came to me, that I could and wanted to translate it, because I have such an affinity for French; I was likewise egged on by my doubt about translation, and in particular about my proficiency therein; I translated the small dialogue at first glance, the way one writes, as it were. It seemed to me that I managed to render the essence of Parny's text—and not at all badly. Hold on! I thought to myself: can you really without any practice whip it off so quickly and intelligibly; let's see if you have any talent, and if Rebecca can do it better; if your version is really better, then you must have talent. My stab at translation was also a sheer challenge I set myself, since there is so much talk these days about translation and I had never tried my hand at it. Well wouldn't you know, my translation is better; so, I do indeed have talent. Should I practice it? Oh, God, I know myself too well! I do have a certain facility; but as soon as I want to refine it, no way! I don't have what it takes to develop my skill. Nature endowed me with much in the way of potential; but all the other gods were absent at my birth.

You ask how I'm doing? The same as always. Do you think I could repeat the same wisecrack I made the last time I visited you—'No wound, but only one fatality you see here before you.' [. . .] I am quiet at the moment, but not yet dead to the world: that's all I can say! But what am I to call that place to which all life is headed and from which it streams forth? And how shall I describe what I see? Despair? God? Another world? Life? Pain? Madness? Punishment? Direction? For me it is all of the above! —And also, a feisty disposition and manner, etc. —I am healthy and weak, and as always, cheerful and lively. But there is no balm to soothe the ache in my heart; that much I know again for sure. Hence this tirade in response to your gentle salutation!

The comb—Don't worry yourself sick about it—I'll send it back to you, precisely because I will gladly accept a gift from you; but I'd like a straight one, without a high plate! From now on I will clearly articulate all my wishes, so that they may be fulfilled, my dear patron saint! Take care of yourself! And don't drink a drop without the OK of that feeble beggar (Dr Böhm). Must you have emotions? Egloffstein should not call on me just to please you. Please tell him that, particularly not at an ungodly hour.

Nothing has happened until it has been talked about at tea

(To Karl Gustav von Brinckmann in Königsberg)

Berlin, 8–9 January 1808
Friday evening, 8 p.m.

Dear Brinckmann! How everything has changed! Oh, dare I say it! If only I were in a state of mind to do so! You are the first person to whom I directed a single word in quite some time—aside from letters to my brother in Hamburg. When I received your last, fourth letter dated 27 November, fever hardly permitted me to read it; my dear, old, true friend, I am still unable to write. Tears well up in my eyes as I write these words. Oh, God, what have I become? Oh, how your letter, your gentle, and therefore painful, letter raised my temperature! [. . .] Nothing has happened until it has been talked about at tea, or written up in the newspaper. I didn't dare write you the most insensible letter; and every amicable word was smothered in my heart; the very thought that the letters would be read made it impossible for me to write. Our mutual friend did indeed bring me your long letter, and promised me an occasion to transmit my reply; but he was not as good as his word [. . .].

At my 'tea table', as you are wont to call it, I sit alone with my dictionaries: tea is no longer prepared here, except for every eight or ten days when Schack, one of the few who did not forsake me, requests a cup. Everything has changed! I never felt so alone. So absolutely alone. Never so totally and utterly bored out of my mind! Just imagine, me bored! For only spirited, amicable, hope-giving words can stave off the malaise of someone as aggrieved, as laid low as I. But it's all behind me now! Last winter, and all the way through to last summer I still frequented a few Frenchmen: with them I chatted of this and that, and we spoke of things that cultivated, literature-loving people not of the same country are able to put into words and hash out. They are all gone now. My German friends, how long has it been since I last saw them; I feel dead to the world, muddled in mind! These days I only still see my second brother, who lives with me at my mother's place, and the foreign gentleman billeted with us. [. . .] (His name is Bribes.) Needless to say, he doesn't speak a word of German; and yet he has a foreign flavour about him, since he comes from that part of France bordering on Spain: pleasant appearance, even of a thoughtful bent, but rather devious, tossed by the tides, rather like a ship; sometimes very distant, then again sometimes close. Our, or should I say, *my* Germanness makes him very suspicious; there appears to be no end to our squabbling over every subject in the world, and all matters of mind! He has a good mind too, but mine appears to perturb him; and it may well be that he takes issue with every woman. So now you have a sense of the man, don't you! He has been living with us going on three months, and there's no telling when he will leave. He is handsome, very natural, never affected. But very thin-skinned; I am ever cautious, always walk on eggshells in his presence. Can you grasp the situation? He hates me a little; and yet he needs me. An unspeakable, inexpressible ennui attests to the extent to which this disturbs me in soul, heart, spirit and what have you! Since, aside from these two people—which is why I tried to describe the stranger to you—him and Madame Frohberg, who is still ill, aside from them I see no one. I did still frequent Pauline until recently, but now she too is gone. All this by word of mouth. I transmit her warm greetings to you.

When, Brinckmann, may I have the pleasure of your company! Or is that not in the cards? Rest assured at the very least, dear friend, that not a word in your four heavenly letters was lost on me; all jest, seriousness, sorrow, all struck a chord in my soul. I am much the same as always, Brinckmann. [. . .] I am still able to share good humour, joy and the greatest distress, but nothing can lay me low, since I am already lying flat. But of one thing I am almost proud. Misfortune has steeled and enshrined that old stubborn streak in me. [. . .] However things turn out, it will not make me change my mind. If I were now seated beside you in an intimate tête-à-tête, I would impart some cheerful chatter about man's essence [. . .] Let us keep still about happenstance that robbed us of friends. [. . .] There's not much that can be changed about our city, much as it changes those who reside here. I always had an inkling of what I previously put in various ways, but now I am absolutely convinced. It [Berlin] is, in any case, perhaps the most ethical place in Europe. [. . .] I saw much of A. Humboldt; but he hardly knows me, and can't abide me; he and Pauline were thick as thieves, but not intimate. A strictly Platonic liaison. Just don't imagine that it was a romantic entanglement!

Friend of the heart, and friend of the mind

(To Pauline Wiesel)

Berlin, 12 March 1811

8.30 p.m., Tuesday

It is an unconscionable scandal that I haven't written to you: a calamity; a calamity like all scandals. Precious, beloved friend of the heart, and friend of the mind! Oh, woe is me!— My heart bleeds! Oh, woe that our life slips away while we live apart. You are alone, separated from me, and I am alone, separated from you. Only once could nature allow two such as us to live in close proximity. Once in this era. Every day in my mind's eye I see you, and me, and the natural bond between us, all the more clearly. Far from you I do nothing but mull over your every word, your every deed, your every remark, and I believe I know the principles by which you live, I know what makes you tick better than you do; there is only one difference between us: you live everything, because you are courageous, and because you were favoured by fortune: I think my way through life, because I was not so favoured in my physique, and because I lack courage; not the courage to wrest good fortune from fate, to wrestle pleasure out of destiny's design; I only acquired the courage to carry myself as I am; but nature made a big mess of us both. And we were born to live truthfully. Each in our own way, we managed to reach the same point. We stand outside society. There is no place, no position, no vain title for the likes of us in this world! All lies amount to much the same; the eternal truth, real living and feeling that tap the deep human potential with which we were endowed is limitless! And that is what excludes us from society, you because you scorned the norm. (I congratulate you for that! You had some compensation: many days of pleasure!) I, because I am constitutionally incapable of sinning and lying comme il faut. I am familiar with your intimate trajectory. Every offence society inflicted on you, albeit sanctioned by the norm, took you by surprise; I could see it coming, step by step. You would gladly have been 'a happy housewife, who cuddles and caresses your man,' as Goethe says in his elegiac couplet; but it wasn't in the cards for you. And where did that terrible store of emotion get you, with all the contrivances of love and life! Not all people are inclined to become self-destructive, self-sacrificing nuns. It's enough to make you want to go to war, me too, to seek to sustain the aspiration with which nature has endowed us to face life. In the name of the eternally just, almighty God seated on his high bench of justice, much less worthy causes have led to war, and been rewarded with medals and honours! Had you but found a warm heart beating in Herr Wiesel's bosom, you would never have sought out another. But given his lack of true feeling and his unfortunate surfeit of words, he groused so much about your untutored and fearful spirit so as to drive you mad. But your superior consciousness held up its own. I know all about it. Your strong heart was not made for suffering. A heart such as yours must have other occupations: so, too, must your eyes, and all your senses. I know what makes you tick: I know you much better, Pauline, than you or anyone might have supposed that one could know someone. You were also quite right about Prince Louis. You know how much I loved him; I still ruminate about him after the fact; 'he altogether lacks generosity of spirit,' you often said. [. . .] But I know what it was in him that really irked you. I understand everything after the fact. He, too, was incapable of sufficiently fathoming what he really wanted, what he really desired so as to act accordingly. [. . .] He was often entwined in momentary whims; and he still believed he had to act in accordance with the image of himself he had drummed into his head 10, 15, 20 years ago, even though he no longer really believed it; or rather, he lacked the courage to show that things had changed in his heart of hearts, that he had since developed other aspirations, other objectives. Consequently, he confounded almost all his hours on earth with his most refined, upright and diligent spirit; and must naturally have inflicted wounds on his dearly beloved at every minute. This finally put you in a state of turmoil, and since the truth in this regard could never be brought to light, a good deal of falsehoods were spoken of you. Only now in retrospect do I realize all this, since I've been tirelessly plummeting my heart and mind, and in the blazing flames of my emotions I fathom ever more. That is how things stand between us; and I cannot come see you at the present time! But I have not given up hope, Pauline, of doing so in the future. I am doing my best to make it happen. But for the moment I have not succeeded. Yet I am hopeful that our plans may be realized. Just imagine, Moritz will probably get married. Whereupon I will once again be all alone on this earth. I have resolved from now on to stop seeing Friedländer—she who changed her name to Frohberg—she's just too insufferable, unnaturally pauvre d'esprit by nature, full of pretensions. I do socialize from time to time, but don't gravitate to a set group of like-minded souls, as in the past. There is not a single soul, either man or woman, with whom I'd be inclined to go for a stroll or attend the theatre. Day by day, I grow ever-more inept at selecting kindred souls. And too proud for friendship. [. . .] Except for the six weeks Moritz spent in Königsberg, he lived the whole winter with me, and still does. I derive little pleasure and much aggravation from his presence. I only exist for him as an afterthought, even though he does see to my pecuniary needs, and is by and large generous. There is another burden on my heart! I still see that young man of whom I wrote you last spring; we go walking in the fields together; I love him with all my heart and soul, am obliged to love him, since his noble qualities demand it. He loves me too; the way one loves the sea, a passing cloud, a ravine. But that's not enough for me. Not any more. Whoever I love must want to live with me; remain by my side. (Campan still writes me love letters, and did so again just recently, inviting me to come.) I will tear this thorn out of my heart, and feel the sharp sting of the wound as it heels and hardens into a scar. And if, like a miserable calling card, 200 Louis d'or lay beside me, I'd hit the road without saying good-bye. All of my friends, except you, think I can live off and pine after the thin air around me. They're glad to watch a game of hearts like mine play itself out, and believe I can live without love! So be it, I've had enough! —One more thing, Pauline! Every day I become more like you. Here and there I still do know some pleasant enough people, but within a week's time I've sounded their depths, and there isn't much there . . . R

Can you tell my mood from this hastily scribbled note?

(To Karl Gustav von Brinckmann in Stockholm)

Berlin, 11 January 1813

Written at 10 a.m. at Behrenstrasse No. 48,

peering out upon snowy streets,

diagonally across from the casino, at street level.

Let this be a hastily scribbled note, since without affixing my soul to paper and blotting out my body, it is impossible for me to draft a proper letter. Too much time has gone by since we were last in touch; too many new, perplexing, big and little things have come to pass for me to tell all, lest I gag in the telling. [. . .] Think of me as more mature, more sophisticated, more crushed in my aspirations, but essentially the same as usual; just give me a breath of fresh air and I'd be contented. I'm in middling health. Not at all under pleasant conditions. I suffer from agoraphobia. I fear the future. So much about me! To which I might add as a postscript of sorts that I am at the moment more ill-prepared and disinclined than ever to write to anyone, and most of all to you; recollecting shared memories of the past engenders an acute paralysis in the present, blocking any subsequent accomplishments; yet to whom else but you can I recount in detail. [. . .] I am neither angry nor surprised that you don't write: a person can only write at length and with pleasure if he can expect a reply that same afternoon. We don't need to reaffirm that we are two of a kind; or else it would not be true at all. Yesterday evening I had tea with the Schleiermachers, whose wife is my dear friend, along with Countess Voss and Herr von Marwitz, the latter my close friend. He is in Potsdam, working at the Chamber of Deputies, and often comes to Berlin. I found Countess Voss to be quite gracious, unpretentious, and quite good looking; I am still immensely fond of her. [. . .] Humboldt hates me again: he passed through Berlin without seeing me. Herz is alive and well and looks as lovely as ever. [. . .] I live alone, October will mark three years since my mother's death. It's been a tough time for me! My sister just has the one child; and I have not seen her for a long time either. Hannchen is a young lady, Fanny still goes to school. They are good, well-behaved children. My brothers are all in Berlin, the youngest married with a young woman from Poland. She is courteous, kind-hearted and innocent. Brought up like the girls here in Berlin. Be well, my friend! And do make plans, when the thunder-storms stop erupting in sentient rain to come to Germany. If between now and then, I should be among those laid low, just think that she was not one of those to whom death came unexpectedly, suffering rather, as she does, from a nameless dread, without any prospect of relief. God protect us! Can you tell my mood from this hastily scribbled note? Adieu! R. R. My last name is Robert now. [. . .]

What is friendship?

(To Friederike Liman in Berlin)

Vienna, Saturday, 4 February 1815

When do we write to our friends? When we want something from them. Who are our friends? The cleverest people who know what friendship is. What is friendship? It is whatever it can be; the ability to see through the facades of other personalities, and the virtue of being able to respect others and to recognize them as independent entities, as we do ourself; the good fortune to have found someone whose nature and sheer being pleases us, in their every expression, in their every action as in each failure; someone who possesses and responds positively to the quality of allowing others to develop freely and to the best of their abilities. Thus, you permit me to remain silent when it would be difficult for me to speak—with tongue or pen—you permit me to whip off a short note that says only that which I wish to say at the present time, what I want from you! That you manage to convince Bethmann—to whom the gist of this entire letter is directed—that for my sake, she receive Brede with all possible courtesy! In word and deed! The fact notwithstanding that she already knows her, and so will surely know what a dear creature she is. Now I demand that she show her the same kindness and conspicuous generosity of spirit with which she once received me when we first met as strangers, and that she grant her the same essential comforting embrace with which she received me and my companions and all Prussians at a difficult and uncertain moment in Prague. Her entire way of being, her focus in life is linked to Berlin, her and our lofty hometown, whose bright spirit radiates above that of all other cities, an unparalleled place, so vaunted on account of its age-old love of art and artists, though Fleck and Iffland be dead. [...]

Vienna is like Leipzig (and less comfortable, on account of its narrow streets and countless carriages. [...] The suburbs are far-flung and uncomfortable, the Prater is no Phoenix,* and it is maddeningly sunny, dusty or mired in the manure of clip-clopping coach horses; of its theatres only those with a comedic focus are up to snuff. Musical comedies are far more popular here than they are in Berlin. [...] That Adamberger woman is such a veritable actrice [...], a pompous fop with a false sounding voice, a noisome jesting manner, a strained highfalutin manner, and not a drop of fresh originality, at least in my view. That in contrast to the big deal they make of her here. [...] I almost never go out to visit. On occasion we do frequent the Arnsteins, and a bit more often the Eskeles:

---

* The Prater is a large public park in Vienna, the site of a famous amusement park. Phoenix is a park in the heart of Dublin conceived in 1751, known as one of the biggest inner-city green spaces in the world.

various gentlemen visit us in the evening. Varnhagen is always home, and I had to make every effort to expand our social connections. People don't stroll around here for pleasure as we do in Berlin; and even riding around in carriages is no fun here. I miss female company. Though this is no doubt my own fault, a function of my difficult character, Vienna may well be a very agreeable place for others. I just don't find it amenable for strolling about. [. . .] Madame Schlegel is invariably very kind, appreciative, droll, mild-mannered, prone to laughter as always; she is pious, but in a way that does not shock me as affectation. He, on the other hand, is insufferable; albeit well disposed towards me. I would surely see her more often if they did not live a bit too far from me, and if they did not have regular house guests, and so, like us, seldom go out, and he were not always home. But I do drop by for an evening every now and then, and weather permitting, on some mornings [. . .] She still loves you all a lot! Asks after you all; remembers everything. [. . .]

I see Frau Frohberg these days only in passing at our salons. A married woman cannot allow herself to be as mistreated as a mademoiselle; otherwise, things would have been as they were before between us. [. . .]

—Let me close with abundant kisses; Varnhagen also sends his warmest greetings, which he insisted I convey forthwith! Write to me of your summer plans, and I will thereafter tell you mine, since I am free to move about as I please. Be well! Adieu! Adieu! [. . .]

So now I know what a congress is:* a large gathering that cannot keep from indulging in various amusements. [. . .] It must surely be downright difficult to run a congress and to end it! To install and configure a whole new world!—such matters made Hamlet melancholic. Now then, let us see if a hero, a seafaring hero cannot let himself be outmanoeuvred. If Wellington will be able to withstand the pressure! What Dresden will reply to Wellington? What is my brother Ludwig up to? His siblings can't squeeze a letter out of him. Why don't you try. Is Tieck in Berlin? 'If only I were a little bird!' Friedrich Schlegel grouses about Goethe. Nevertheless, he stays in Vienna, and grows ever-more stupid.

---

* A reference to the Congress of Vienna (1814–1815), the international diplomatic meetings to discuss the future of Europe following the defeat of Napoleon. Rahel joined her husband, who was a member of the delegation from Prussia.

Do you know that peculiar kind of melancholy?

(To Friedrich Ludwig Lindner)

Karlsruhe, Wednesday morning, 29 April 1818
Warm weather of blossoming trees,
the air atwitter with birdsong.

Do you know that peculiar kind of melancholy, a forward surge, a pretension, an expectation of the impending, an acute premonition, particularly in such weather? And a peering inwards into oneself and all that one has lived through [. . .] That is how I'm feeling [. . .] So today, of all days, I should not ordinarily have written to you; but your letter that arrived the day before yesterday demands a written response, come what may. How happy it made me, that letter of yours; and not just because it was addressed to me, not just because of all the flattering things you say about me; what pleased me above all is that it is such an endearing, honest, eloquent letter. [. . .] Everything about it, its tone, the expressions you employed, conjures up your physiognomy [. . .] You will, I'm quite sure, have disabused yourself of the dubious notion that I am some kind of towering intellect in the course of our conversation, of that I am quite certain. [. . .] Come soon, and stay as long as you like [. . .]

I consider this name change to be of pivotal importance

(To Ernestine Goldstücker in Berlin)

Karlsruhe, 16 May 1818

—I consider this name change to be of pivotal importance. To a certain extent, in so doing you become, outwardly at least, another person; and this is particularly necessary. —I am very happy that Beguelin will be your baptismal godparent; do not tarry in making all arrangements as soon as possible. You will, I assume, also have your children baptized along with you. They have already been raised as Christians; and they must, insofar as possible, not hear anything more about that mad historical fluke,* than they would of history itself! —But you have absolutely no reason to adhere to the faith into which you were born. You must also conform externally to your class, adhering in custom, views, culture and convictions to that class of persons to which you belong. You will thereby controvert the sole detrimental tendency to which this adherence leans, namely, the recent outburst of hatred of the Jews; the deplorable vestiges (I am inclined to think of them as warning signs for nation builders) of a great and gifted

_____

* Presumably a derogatory reference to Judaism.

78

nation otherwise so Godfearing and advanced in matters of faith; so humane, i.e. Christian, individually and en gros; individually by imparting their most laudable convictions; en gros, when, under pretence of promoting their Christian faith, they mistreat a group of people, instead of trying to win them over through kind-hearted, magnanimous behaviour, simply because they happen to reside in a Christian state. You have no cause to be ashamed of your Jewish birth, and to relinquish your connection to a nation whose misfortune and failings you know all too well, just so that it not be said of you that you still have something Jewish about you! Let yourself be emboldened by your newfound faith, not to pay heed to such prejudices! Speak with Beguelin in general about your attitudes, tell him and me about your life, so that he may know you, and so that he may more joyfully, confidently and willingly take on your sponsorship, so that your life may take on a vibrant purpose, and that you find a true friend, one to whom you may confide and confess, and who, in turn, may offer you consolation and advice. It is possible to enliven one's life; and I am all for it; this is life's greatest joy, and in my view, life's primary purpose.

I do want a letter to be a portrait of
the moment in which it was written

(To Konrad Engelbert Oelsner in Paris)

Berlin, Thursday, 10 p.m., 27 December 1821

Here in Berlin, we are still experiencing a thawing of the ice and snow, without it ever having completely frozen over; once on the eighth of this month, snow fell without sticking to the ground; at midday every day the sun makes an effort to shine; as to the stars come evening, you can see them flicker in the sky. 'Italy!' people cry out: they mean the weather.

You told me how you found my notes about the weather; I'll tell you why I make such notes. Precisely for the opposite reason than the chemists of whom you speak do so. In following weather conditions, they seek to establish the method by which they think they proceed; but I do so to help excuse my unmethodical manner. The weather helps set the stage for the day, indeed, the day's essential layout is in part prescribed by it; and if my reader assimilates the day's physiognomy, as I fancy portraying its physiognomic features, he will more readily grasp the irregularity of my manner of speaking, and it will at least put it in a context. My manner of writing is not altogether involuntary. I do want a letter to be a portrait of the moment in which it is written; and it succeeds, in my estimation, principally depending on how much it accords with the ideal artistic demands of the form, demands the letter writer must take into account, but blind adherence to which yields an affected and empty result. There are methodical, measured spirits not lacking in substance who just need to let themselves go, and always need to show themselves with the best face forward. Those are the happy ones; they suffer from no moodiness, no bad weather! Or rather, their moods are a music of the finest tuning; and their weather condition is set by the sun that shines through the purest, mildest air.

Time flies

(To Auguste Brede in Stuttgart)

Monday, 6 January, 9 p.m.

Bitter cold; one thousand, eight hundred and twenty-three.

It flies; but only over our heads, on our heads it wipes its lower claws and paws, and often more than wipes; it clobbers, belts, scratches and wounds, and keeps pressing down on us almost constantly—I am talking about time; that fleeting thing that only matters for poor people; that construct; which is why I, too, chide it today in flight. Gladly, dearest Auguste, would I write you something nice; really and truly would I do so now to gladden and regale you. But nothing comes to mind. For more than eight days, twelve indeed, I believe, I haven't gone out: because the weather gives me a cramp in the chest: which is why I don't hear or see much. But which makes me all the more receptive to all the details you give me about your life, you, my steadfast and best friend! [. . .]

There is only one person in this world
who knows who I really am

(To Pauline Wiesel in Paris)

Berlin, Sunday, Noon,

5 November 1826.

Unseasonably warm, hazy weather,

where the sun breaks through the cloud cover.

Dear heart! My one and only Pauline! She who must stay
alive, or else I'd be so lonesome, I might as well be buried in
my grave! There is only one person in this world who knows
who I really am. Her, her, her! No one will believe it: I know
it's true. And to this one and only, to you, I refrain from
writing. Oh, it's only natural. I'd have to write with my life-
blood, rather than ink; that's what I'd have to do: I'd have to
tap so deep in my veins it would completely wipe me out: and
you already know everything: everything about me, except the
things one experiences living together: the most sensual details
of the present moment, the now of now. So, listen up, my
painfully honest, my one and only Pölle! I received the dear
innocent love letter you sent me this summer after Mama's
death, in which you proposed a rendezvous at your expense.
My faithful Pauline, I would gladly have accepted if it were

only a matter of money, if you had enough to cover the cost. It was just not possible, on account of Varnhagen's responsibilities and needs; and also, on account of my very compromised health last summer: this 'not' is enough, *was* unfortunately enough to make travel impossible. That's why I postponed writing you; and so, I am ashamed to say, it took me till now. But here, now, a word about plans I hope to put into action! My entire plan, all my efforts are geared to spending some time with you in the country some time next summer. [. . .] I live quite constrained, not on account of lack of funds, but rather due to a dearth of people who mean much to me, and because I am in a relationship, and every relationship is emotionally draining. Adieu, dear heart! Varnhagen is not home, and doesn't know that I'm writing to you, or else he would surely send greetings. He is generous of spirit, as you well know, and still as kind and understanding as always. My niece's four children—the oldest four years old—are still staying with us. I also frequent actresses—foreigners and locals: Madame Neumann from Karlsruhe; Mlle. Pfeiffer from Munich; Madame Stich from here. Please reply to this letter, my precious Pölle! I'm going to stop by for a visit to Markus, who isn't well; I'm not feeling up to snuff myself, but I am alert. The thought of you refreshes me. I will go visit your sister one of these days, she sent me her address. We've engaged Dore's sister as our cook, and she prepares splendid dishes. Please reply in detail! Addio, cara, cara, my one and only.

My prison of sickness, suffering and melancholy

(To Princess Lucie von Pückler-Muskau in Berlin)

Sunday, 19 December 1830

At the first breakthrough ray of sunlight today I hope to attempt an escape from my prison of sickness, suffering and melancholy, from that unrejuvenated morass, that muddle of English fog and mist; to flee from a grey on grey, colourless, formless confinement; without gasping for air! I want to pull out in a proper carriage; but my legs are still too weak to let me climb in and out of a buggy, tackle stairs, trade the familiar air of room and hallway for the unfamiliar; or else I would inquire if your serene Highness might countenance a visit!

As such, however, given my lingering condition, I ask for form's sake, if you are well. I have heard that His Highness, Prince Pückler, is not up to snuff. I hope that he, too, does not suffer from nightlong insomnia, the bane of my existence, to mention only one complaint. I am obliged to refrain from coffee, tea, beer and wine. Without a dash of indulgence, I could never fall asleep; the consequent ennui drains all my reserves of spirit! Do you no longer go out in the evening? Or am I out of favour? I think not, but if so, I recommend myself for clemency; permit me to ingratiate myself with a selection of newspapers. Here at tea, you will find the latest French headlines! I urge Your Highness to take the air; it does a body well! Just don't make too many house calls; keep the outings outside, as it were. Here's hoping and believing that I may soon hear from you. Please also extend best wishes to His Highness, the Prince.

Respectfully as ever, your devoted friend,

Frau Varnhagen.

IV

GRAPPLING WITH GOETHE

AND OTHER CONTEMPORARY AUTHORS OF NOTE,

AND OTHER LITERARY REFLECTIONS

In 1795, on a sojourn in the spa town of Karlsbad, Rahel, then age 24, was introduced to the illustrious poet, playwright and thinker, Johann Wolfgang von Goethe (1749–1832), almost twice her age. Goethe was greatly impressed by her original bent of mind, describing her in a letter to his daughter-in-law, Ottilie von Goethe, as 'a beautiful soul'. In awe of the illustrious author and his writings, Rahel and her husband, Karl August, later engaged in an exchange of letters concerning Goethe's work, which Varnhagen published in 1812 in the journal *Morgenblatt für gebildete Stände*. Excerpts from this correspondence, as well as her letters to other authors of note, including one drafted but never sent to French novelist, playwright and poet, Victor Hugo (1802–85), as well as some of her journal reflections on writing and literature, are included here.

Man is himself a work of art

(To Karl Gustav von Brinckmann in Berlin)

Paris, early 1801

Man is himself a work of art, and his entire being consists therein that consciousness and un-consciousness alternately hold sway. That is why I love Goethe so much, and why I maintain that the poet as artist must tap his entire temperament—like the sculptor his marble—and in a certain sense, the poet always desecrates himself; so long as he succumbs to the yoke of his own suffering, he is no poet; he only becomes a true poet, strictly speaking, when he embraces his all-suffering sentiments; this alternation is recorded with such precision by the great Goethe that he elicits tears of admiration—and is admiration not the most genuine emotion, a sentiment matched only by sympathy? Why do we favour above all the harmonious development of our faculties, and yet not permit ourselves the complete panoply of feeling?—Why should the poet ultimately restrict himself to tap only a lyrical vein? There can be no harmony in a single voice. The fact that this man simply must be a poet is constraint enough:

everything else about him must be a function of free will, that is how this artist mimics humanity, and it is this alone, this alternation between the dominance of the conscious and the unconscious mind that makes him a poet! And with what stirring integrity Goethe manages to do just that! This is my eternal refrain. The same is true with love, the experience of which is by far not as natural as it is made out to be; first I feel that I can love, then that I want to love, then that I must love. This gives rise to a fervent passion—it is a human, all-too-human progression—based on the same fluctuation. He who can depict it is a poet; he who can feel it is a lover; he who can explain it, break it down to its constituent parts, is a philosopher. How often are these three stages grossly muddled in a person and in our assessment of a person?

Does it surprise you that I can pray to God? Does our reflection concerning ourselves and our lot not often go so far that we find no proof for our existence, and are obliged to resort to feeling: does that not amount to self-worship? When the need to understand is most intense, we feel the presence of God, and then we pray! Herein lies the difference; here at the end of all that is perceptible, we are compelled to recognize Him, dolorous and prodigious, but always the same: we must recognize His existence, even if we don't sense it at every moment. It is surely not a human being; it is surely not a thinking person unable to detect the shift between consciousness and the unconscious. Schiller calls this the break. It is our task in life to consciously or unconsciously dissolve this break.

We cannot predict if this dissolution will make us happy: for such is our limitation, we are only half-conscious in our displeasure; the religious are satisfied without consciousness; those who find happiness in conscious reflection I would call pious.

Throughout my life this poet has led me unerringly
and helped me realign what misfortune and good fortune
had shattered

(To Karl August Varnhagen von Ense in Berlin)

Berlin, 22 July 1808

You cannot imagine with what a fright I woke up! A debilitating train of thought leading nowhere pressed heavy on my heart. So, I remained lying in bed, undecided, ever vacillating; for don't I know all too well the way things are, and that nothing can ever be resolved? I lay there in a bundle of fear. I thought I ought to write you about it, took the volume of Goethe's works in hand and went downstairs. The book lay beside me, and I, in despair, beside it! Ordinarily it would be a festive occasion to have in hand a new volume of Goethe's writings; every bundle of his words is a charming, lovely, beloved, honoured guest that promises to open new gates of perception to new, heretofore unknown facets of life. Throughout my life, this poet has accompanied me unerringly and with a strong hand guided me in good health and helped me realign what misfortune and good fortune had riven, an emotional divide that I evidently was not otherwise able to hold together. I kept company with his wealth of images and ideas, he was always my one true friend; my guarantor that I not worry myself to death in the grip of divisive tendencies; my sage master, my most heartfelt friend, who kept no secret of the abysses to which he himself had descended!—in short, I grew up with him, and after a thousand separations I invariably found him again, he was always there for me; and since I am not myself a poet, I will never be able to find the words to express what he meant to me! And yet the very thought of him and his words moves me to tears! [. . .] A kind of fear that fed my inattentiveness kept me from opening the book; I feared that I might no longer find my way back to him and to myself in this text. I also wanted to write to you about this inability as a sign of my decline, my grief, my being broken; and I was so consumed by my fear, my paralysis and my pain that I could not write a word. Entrapped in this paralysis of mind, my pain bore no fruit! My friend, my one and only true friend lay there beside me, but we both were dead, dead! My breakfast was a bit slow in coming, and then all of a sudden, my fear abated, so that I was finally able to pick up the book. And so, I read on, lacking courage and hope—and find in his words exactly what I myself am feeling! Read the prelude! [. . .]

> They still are moved at once to weeping or to laughter,
> Still wonder at your flights, enjoy the show they see:
> A mind, once formed, is never suited after;
> One yet in growth will ever grateful be.*

---

* Johann Wolfgang von Goethe, 'Prelude at the Theatre' in *Faust, Part One* (Bayard Taylor trans., 1871[1808]).

Yet again, my friend found the words for what I was feeling! Nevermore will I despair! Judge for yourself how at this very moment his words move me! He reawakened all of my gratitude, all of my tender feelings. I had to relate this to you more or less the way I experienced it. And now that that is behind me, my heart falls shut again. Let me read on. [. . .]

No one can love me without loving Goethe

(To Karl August Varnhagen von Ense in Berlin)

Hamburg, 30 October 1808

If I once told you that there was a deep, unreachable reservoir of feeling inside me, I did not thereby mean to suggest that it was grounded in my spirit and that it could not be reached. But rather, that I believe that there is in my spirit something inaccessible to other people; and that everyone carries around inside himself just such a dowry of strangeness; I just happened to become conscious of it. No one person can mimic the way the spirit and its concomitant doubt can shake up another person—that is what I meant, and that is what I must make clear to you. Love cannot sound these depths, though it flows into all the other component parts of our being [. . .] How blissful it makes me to read in your letter what you write of Goethe! How delighted I am, how your admiration for the master soothes my heart! It is the greatest guarantee, the greatest proof that you love me. Oh, no one can love me without loving Goethe: he is the ideal, the essence of life itself evoked by concrete means. That is why I am so terribly aggrieved when people speak badly of him. I will never renounce my attachment to him; if I said so myself then it must be someone else speaking in my stead, then I would have to metamorphose from the tree of knowledge into the insidious snake! [. . .] His words read altogether like a translation to me; not as if the text itself were translated; but therein lies his mastery, his ability to grasp the way of life of the French, to fathom their language so as to be able to render expression down to the most minute shift of sentence structure, and thereby for his connoisseurs to be and to remain the one and only Goethe! [. . .] It pleases my soul that he should remind you of Diderot.

A sense of place

(To Karl August Varnhagen von Ense in Berlin)

Hamburg, 6 November 1808

Concerning the depiction of places, you and I have an alto-gether different standpoint. There is a profound difference between evocation and description, and the poet is obliged to alternately do one and then the other. In your letters from Dresden, for instance, you offered a divine description of the bridge. And should you ever wish to describe a bridge in a poem, you'd be hard pressed to do any better. Herr Goethe, however, in the entirety of his epic poem, *Hermann und Dorothea*, without consciously intending to do so, from the first line to the last, so precisely depicts a region, a day, the weather, local conditions and the pace of passing time, that it becomes an essential element in the poem, which helps to make the reader perceive it as an actual day in an actual place. No one has ever remarked upon this in print. Whoever fails to see the place of which Goethe is speaking must surely lack the camera obscura, of which Jean Paul speaks; and Goethe has arranged things such that the latter might indeed be missing, and the only person who doesn't see it is he who, having been taken to said place twice in succession, can be convinced they are two different places.

His original language was lost

(Journal notation)

A quiet Friday, 20 April 1821

In the Biblical story of Adam, it is said that his original language was lost. We are only still able to ascribe very shadowy, cursory qualities of things with our language; we have no other means at our disposal in our soul to probe or to reply. It is no empty expression when we say in German 'it wants to rain, lightning wants to strike', etc. What we, in fact, mean is that no movement is possible unless it is willed. Even though we cannot even say of ourselves how we came to want what we want, how we arrived at the fundamental will underlying our wanting. An even greater evidence that there is a primordial will out of which derives our basic volition [. . .]. A single great music of will. That is how I interpret Friedrich Schlegel when he recently declared in Frankfurt that fire is a spirit. Fire wants something in particular: it is as if it had, or it is a mandate of the highest will: as are all spirits, and everything distilled to its spiritual essence. We are more conscious of our innermost aspiration than we are of its limitations, condition and connection; and it is one of the most maddening, prevalent errors that we ordinarily believe that we know more about our body than we do about our spirit; we suffer more corporeally, since in relation to our body we appear to possess a less active will, and know even less about its qualities [. . .] So, too, do things stand with human interaction. The less well we know a spirit the more it is a matter of concern, an indecipherable matter for us. Recognition is progress, life, higher engagement, comprehension of volition and of augmented existence.

The French and the Germans
are like two halves of a whole

(Dialogue recorded by Karl August Varnhagen von Ense)

Sunday, 23 March 1823

In a conversation about the book *Des hommes célèbres de France au dix-huitième siècle, et de l'état de la littérature et des arts à la même époque* by Johann Wolfgang von Goethe, Rahel said:

R. The French and the Germans actually belong together, like two halves of a whole; Englishmen seem to me to be altogether different; they are rather like a variation of Germans.

A. Swedes and Danes too. How different and distinctive, on the other hand, are Spaniards; a splendid nation! So level-headed! A level-headed people is to be admired.

R. Indeed, their great wit and their sensibility delight me: I don't mean what we generally mean by wit; but rather, the wit of their poetry, their literature. A people can only be judged according to its literature. How cultivated they must be and their conviviality! And the French and the

Germans do, after all, have the greatest literature; that is why they fit together and act as a counterweight to each other.

A. One cannot judge a people solely based on its literature; their character is also a decisive factor. For instance: the Russians. What character! And they have no literature at all.

R. They are also non-European. And they and all peoples seek our cultivation, and strive after it; indeed, I can conceive of cultivated peoples without literature, but they have to be altogether different, their cultivation must have been absorbed into life; movement as in dance; and with altogether different institutes and intents [. . .]—but the Danes, Swedes, Russians all want what we want; and newer peoples can only be judged based on their literature.

A. Yes, in a situation in which the individual is completely consumed by his nation!

R. No, in which the nation lives in each individual!

A. That too! [. . .]

R. That too? What then is a nation? [. . .] if each bird could fly on its own, the flock would not be necessary.

Pondering the extraordinary individual
who in a wondrous way expresses herself in these pages

(Letter from Johann Wolfgang von Goethe to Ottilie von Goethe)

13 August 1824

I have taken to heart and to mind the noteworthy excerpts from the letters and loose pages you left for me, though I haven't yet actually read through them, I could not immediately find time. But since they lay beside me long enough and I often glanced in their direction, each time pondering the extraordinary individual who wrote them, and who in a wondrous way expresses herself in these pages, I was finally inclined to consider, from beginning to end, the extraordinary life journey such a person must have gone through to suffer and survive such contingencies. You will, my dear, have to extend my heartfelt thanks. I already had a certain sense of this person and the conditions of her life, a picture that has now been fleshed out; but, in fact, everything I read relating to this person was new and striking.

Can one make a clean break from what one actually is?

(Letter from Rahel to Ottilie von Goethe)

September 1824

Can one make a clean break from what one actually is; a complete break: like a fragile little vessel driven by wind and storm far out to sea! [. . .] As soon as I read your precious letter, I had an answer ready. What could be more precious, more valuable to me than your note with the cited lines from your father-in-law. He read my letter. Were it not for your intercession, he never would have laid eyes on my words, let alone read them. I am all too well aware of that, you cannot imagine how much emotion I felt at your transmission of his response. But as some pious people inflict pain on themselves to demonstrate to their God what they can and want to do for Him, for the first time I let myself gush about myself and about things that matter most to me. [. . .] And I must ask you not to forget, indeed to take into consideration, that much is excerpted from narrative references, from informal, comic, annoying, anguished letters written long ago from different times in my life; and that only this excerpted passage, in the context in which it appears, can vouchsafe and entertain diversion. To this very day I am vexed by those who do not know what they are going to say, people not lacking in judgement and discretion, who do not handle said judgements well, but rather are handled by them. How ashamed I am, how hideous I seem to myself to spot off as I am doing here; what I so despise in others, and what I have tried to avoid for my entire life. Il faut aussi passer par là!* That is a bitter transition, but at least I didn't stand in the way. I just want to have said this to you. Since receiving your letter, this seemed essential, the most important thing. [. . .]

Each person's life unravels more or less the same way. My deepest wish for you is that your life remain as far removed as possible from this errant way. May the greatest self-composure become your greatest leisure activity. May the most pure, inner harmony bring about an outer serenity. [. . .] If, come winter, you think of us in Berlin, please accept my best wishes for all that is desirable for your wonderful family; let domestic bliss sweeten your longings. [. . .]

---

* You also have to go through this.

Unlike every other spoken word,
the lie does not unfetter the constricted chest

(Journal notation, 18 March 1825)

Has there ever been a more splendid saying conceived to combat the lie, a sounder dictum for the truth, more naive, more attuned to nature, than this: 'Unlike every other sincerely spoken word, the lie does not unfetter the constricted chest!' from Goethe's *Iphigenia*. Let us also venerate the common German saying that expresses much the same: 'You lie down your throat!'

Goethe's pen

(Journal notation)

Friday, 8 July 1825

On Friday evening, at around 8.45 p.m., on 8 July 1825, Goethe gave me a quill pen with the assurance, to which he could swear, that he used it to write with on that very day!!! This is how it came to pass: I asked Frau von Goethe to steal such a pen for me; but she proved a faulty thief: the father saw her do it, whereupon he had a quill still fresh with ink, accompanied by the aforementioned words, sent to the vestibule where I waited. I'll say no more about it! Let it be henceforth recognized and acknowledged by all as Goethe's pen.

A literary style is only good if, like the skin of a fruit,
it grew out of the innermost core

(Journal reflection)

7 October 1825

A literary style is only good if, like the skin of a fruit, it grew out of its innermost core. Nothing dead, nothing fabricated, nothing superimposed should be noticeable. The same holds true for forms of verse. Every person is a completely unique specimen, altogether singular in gifts, and in his perception of the universe, of things and thoughts; even if we seem so similar; that's why we're here! And that is the special something, the potential in each of us that we have to offer the world; and the more developed, the more beautiful it is!

Do not, I beg you, count me among the scribblers of note

(To Friedrich de la Motte Fouqué in Nennhausen)

Berlin, Wednesday, 17 June 1829

God be with you, dear Baron Fouqué. Here's wishing you courage, that is to say, patience, in your indisposition! My own malaise is still so fresh and present that I still know all too well how courage and patience help you get through it. And how sick I was, how much at odds I was with the earth I stand on and the atmosphere I breathe! Only two entities were apprised of my condition: God almighty and myself; and now only one, namely, Him. One can endure the worst of it, but not keep it bottled up in the soul. My patience consisted therein never to fully grasp the extent of my malaise; but rather, to experience it misery by misery, pain by pain, minute by minute. A kind of animal-like, childish innocence dictated my behaviour; a quality you will not be lacking! That is what I wanted to tell you: and that is why I salute you now with all my heart. Here's hoping that you are now feeling much better in your heart, your soul and your spirit; and convalescing in midsummer on your lovely country estate, surrounded by your loved ones, and keeping busy; I'm quite sure you're on the mend. Still suffering from frazzled nerves and rheumatism, I am otherwise doing well. And you will, I'm quite sure, enjoy a speedy recovery; soldiers like you can't abide being laid up too long.

Do not, I beg you, count me among the scribblers of note! Not that I would not willingly, all-too-gladly call myself a writer. I would not be ashamed to draft a Newtonian treatise on astronomy, or a mathematical work; but not having been able to author a single coherent work, I shy away from condoning that my words appear in print. But not being able to produce a single coherent work, I am loath to publish anything. I wish you well, dear Baron! And hope that next winter will find you better able to brave the elements; here's hoping that you might also find a snippet of time to spend with us. With best regards to Madame von Fouqué, I wish you a productive summer. Your humble servant,

Fr. V.

*Words are pearls compressed for a half century
and spit up out of a stormy human soul*

(To Antonie Theodora von Horn in Berlin)

Sunday, 11 October 1829

My well-disposed and most talented friend! You yourself may
gauge how much your writing gladdens my heart from this
brief accounting of the genesis of what you just read. Although
I have hardly written a word in many years, even Voltaire and
others like him didn't fire off more letters and notes than I did
early on in my life. But back then I didn't know what I was
doing; and had I sought some explanation, it would have been
this: all people write as much as and whatever they feel
inclined to write. I lived in this cloud of innocence* up until
the last days of my youth; even though in the early days of my
adolescence, up until my twelfth and thirteenth year, my little
handwritten notes and letters to my siblings stirred up a good
bit of laughter and wisecracks, I was firmly convinced—thank
God!—that this was on account of the miscomprehension of

---

* *Unschuldswetter*, literally 'the weather of innocence', a term coined by
Rahel to denote a condition of 'utter innocence'. Rahel kept a record of
weather conditions to which she ascribed a powerful effect on the psyche.

the recipients, the fact that they were so dense, they didn't get what I meant; and also because I wasn't able to express myself clearly, convinced as I was that everyone was just like me and thought just like me. For the longest time, shamefully long, I was convinced of this, though in each case, I came to recognize in what ways we differed. Such was my good fortune, my singular and greatest joy. Ever since my youth, my mind has seethed with notions of the truth; nature landed sharp and telling stings on my sharp sensory organs; I was born with a rock-solid, sensitive heart that forever and forthrightly enlivened all the other organs; my head was inclined to deeper deliberation and understanding; I had almost no external grace. Consequently, I had to drink up all the goblets and chalices of experience, however bitter and sharp, down to their dregs; I was spared no blow of a club, no prick of a needle, no nail, no snag of a hook; no accidental slipup; a double-slipup, because I did not always recognize it as such; and if I recognized it, I did not always repel it. In short, I got my grounding in the school of hard knocks; and these bon mots taken from a heap of letters and from a few diaries—collected by Varnhagen—are the product of silent, long-lived, long-ignored pains, tears, suffering, brooding; the fruit of solitude and consequence of breaks in the never-ending ennui. Pearls compressed for a half century and spit up out of a stormy human soul, treasures of the kind dredged from the deep [...]

What demon of inspiration took root in your soul!

(To Victor Hugo; written in Berlin, April 1831)

Surely, Monsieur, the feeling of gratitude to a veritable genius who has elevated your soul, touched your heart, stunned your imagination and satisfied that innate moral fibre at the core of our being is not unknown to you; geniuses have also delighted you—you have loved them—as you well know, when one is so favourably disposed one would like to see those one admires admired and applauded by others, and revered as we revere them, or one would like to prove to others that they were understood, appreciated by an intelligence that grasped or suspected their meaning. It is that feeling of almost tormented admiration that at the moment almost erases in me that sense of an inferior and frail personality. It is a German woman who writes to you, Monsieur, after having read *Notre Dame de Paris*. What a completely original concept of a book! What demon of inspiration took root in your soul! It is as if you took possession of that masterpiece of architecture! You extracted the soul of the sanctuary Notre Dame de Paris; and that, in my view, is the great merit

---

Drafted in French, this letter to the great French novelist was never completed and never sent.

of your novel, a completely new vantage point. While I did not understand anything in the first volume, I was furious with you, not seeing any character emerge, and that is precisely what I admire most today. Your book is itself like a great masterpiece of Gothic architecture that our little imagination does not immediately comprehend—spoilt as it is by an atmosphere of prejudice in which it lives. —And like those other great architectural poems, your poem is a veritable construct, in which the grandest presupposes the most minute, they are both part of the same life. That is the impression I am left with after finishing reading the book. That then is how I see it all, grasp the entirety of it [. . .] and such is the effect of all that is true, conceived in the innocence and integrity of our spirit. All those who still possess that innocence and who stand alone in their assessment of a book will love *Notre Dame* and its author. There are in Germany more such fortunate souls than you might perhaps imagine, and it behoves one of us to sacrifice his vanity and pretend to have much to make you know this posterity that lives beside you: for strangers are a bit like those who come after us. Truly great men surely put little store in the praise of such posterity: but they love to do good for the entire human species. So, I am pleased to tell you how much you are admired in Germany, that you are revered and appreciated here. Germany is a country with no centre, no Paris [. . .]; but all over Germany there are souls open to all beautiful genres, souls on the lookout that merit admiration; without, however, possessing the grace that renders a cult agreeable to God—

The poet

(Selected journal notations)

A poet is a person in whom all strings on which experience plays are plucked, whereupon they vibrate; but what of those in whom such strings are absent!

*

Herein lies the principal difference between the poet and the liar: the former cannot tell a lie without an underlying grain of truth, and the latter cannot tell the entire truth without a backdrop of lies.

*

There are privileged souls, regal spirits who remain innocent for a long time, who can never quite manage to grasp crude insult and always promptly forget it.

V

LETTERS TO AND RECOLLECTIONS OF

CONVERSATIONS WITH

KARL AUGUST VARNHAGEN VON ENSE

In the summer of 1803, Rahel met Karl August Varnhagen von Ense, 14 years her junior, at the home of Philippine and Eduard Cohen, where he was engaged at the time as a private tutor to the Cohen children. They met again in 1808 and married in 1814. Following a brief career in the military, Varnhagen entered the Prussian civil service and held various diplomatic positions. The couple resided thereafter in Vienna, Frankfurt am Main, Mannheim and Karlsruhe, wherever Varnhagen was posted, before returning in 1819 to Berlin. Following her death in 1833, he devoted the rest of his days to collecting and publishing her letters and promoting her reputation.

Do you see the rain?

Thursday, 12 May 1808

Do you see the rain? It is a perfectly ordinary downpour that then runs ragged in the wind. Let us derive a proper pleasure from the trip we intended to take today; let us delight in it all till the drops dry up in the sun and leave us milder weather. You are coming here, I hope; I intend to stay in the city, or nearby, the weather is surely good enough for that. Just don't waver; that's why I'm writing you, so that you don't show up at five o'clock. But not at a thousand o'clock either.

Here, my dear, take this flask!

Wednesday, 17 August 1808

Here, my dear, take this flask; I've lugged it around for quite some time; and I didn't give it to you right away, because its stopper case was a bit bashed in; this morning I went looking to buy another, but emerging (languid after my bath), went running around in vain among the shops in our neighbourhood; such unsightly goods are not to be had for time or money.

I'm not giving it to you as a keepsake, as people are inclined to call it: I can't abide keepsakes. How dissimilar will be the moment of my giving it to you and the moment it reminds you of me. Keepsakes are embarrassing and often disconcerting. I'm giving it to you, because I'd really like to provide, obtain and offer you everything! If in the near future I manage to find a more fetching flask, we'll swap them. Did you sleep? Are you well? I caress you with my brown and blue hands! You rascal! Adieu, my love! R. L.

I am a misbirth, and ought to be highborn

Thursday, 27 February 1812

[. . .] I left this letter lying around so as to first have another one from you; I've had bad luck with letters to you that have to run after you: I was also too much under the weather, too unhappy, too bored to write. I am alone without being able to read, this has been my state for the last three days—unable to tolerate the company of other people, and dissatisfied with my siblings. Without air, music, without anything worth looking at out the window, or just—enough said. Without any hope of a gratification or amusement; dreading the summer; and drowning in a great sea of countless drops of failure. Without recourse to madness, or to another world, since this world is as good as any other. In short, I find myself in a state of the most tiresome despair! It's taking too long; whether as a test of my mettle, penance for my faults, or what have you. It's too much to bear for a high-strung creature like myself. —Words fail me! I have finally found the courage to put an end to it all. Only the thought of it keeps me from carrying it out: that one does so much in spite of oneself; I have no more expectations from this life. I cannot imagine anything more miserable than to wait it out till age 60, hoping things will be different. —I find it gradually more and more difficult to get through every successive événement! And not a soul can tell me: do this or do that; there's nothing to be done about it. She's doing fine, under the circumstances, they all think in a fuzzy, unclear way; so much for those who loathe me the least. Friends just shrug their shoulders. If I shot myself, they would be surprised, as they were about Kleist. At least I did not evince surprise at his funeral, insofar as I kept the faith!

You are the only person I've met on this earth who senses and knows the truth, and for whom it is clear in what a God-awful state I'm in. I found no answers to all of life's demands on my nature. Ever. You were smitten by this realization, and that is a big part of your love for me. I'm playing out this wretched charade for your eyes only!

Had you yourself killed me, and an incorporeal conscience of the act still hovered in the terrestrial realm, I would embrace you with all my love, as I do now. I have wanted to tell you that for a long time; and now at long last my debt of gratitude comes due; I often feel more loving than I am at present, in my sickened and sorry state, able to express. As you well know. And this amorous root bore loving branches, and also some blossoms. If it was vanity, then my vanity manifested itself in the thought: he will treat me differently than all the other women; attraction appears to draw him to me; and none of the others suited him. As a friend, I also stand high above all the rest. And it is more tolerable for me not to be your best loved woman—you don't need a best loved—but rather to know that your love, which I don't deserve, belongs to me. [. . .] You are also mistaken, my dear friend, and definitely are far from the truth when you maintain: 'We live unattentively through the years of our youth, and find ourselves unexpectedly transformed from a good child into a rascal.' A child is an undeveloped, untouched thing, and is always good, because his bluster is directed against table, chair and plaything, which we readily concede to him, and the destruction of which we don't hold against him; thus, the child is not *bad*, at least for lack of a more precise characterization! But the years of one's youth are the most virtuous, beautiful, fieriest; so, I definitely do not pardon youth for any villainy. It can only lead to an addled product if the highest fermentation produces nothing but sludge. Tempestuous youth can definitely be reckless, but only to itself. [. . .]

My dear good friend! Your letter to Goethe about me alarms me quite a bit. Naturally he will deem your assessment a consequence of youth and love. You speak of my 'talent'?! Do I possess a nameable talent? Other than the ability to grasp life; and sometimes to present what I see in a baroque, comic or tragic husk. My misfortune—as I have maintained for a long time—to my eternal shame, remains untitled; which is why no one can ever help me. I am a misbirth, and ought to be highborn, ought to have a lovely husk to cover my fruitful core! You should rather have written him of my many contacts and acquaintances. That's what he asked about; and he did indeed observe, him being an observer par excellence, that I must be such a person. But be that as it may, if he ever does see me, he will immediately grasp what's cooking in me. Adieu. And, meanwhile, be well!

Sometimes the sun shines, sometimes it doesn't

Baden, near Vienna, 2 July 1815

Sometimes the sun shines, sometimes it doesn't, following a heavy downpour. Yesterday I went with Jettchen Ephraim and Frau von Münk, an Englishman, a Frenchman, and other companions from Rauneck to visit a high mountain covered with ruins, among them a square tower, the interminable steps of which I proceeded to climb. The view from above was divine. All around me, as far as the eye could see, horizon beyond horizon, I witnessed the most unbelievable spectacle, the sky flashing from dark to light, over shimmering fields of grain, over the Schwechat River, which like an animal sniffed at the valley below, and turned to rush past countless villages and properties, towards dark, headstrong mountains. Sheep were grazing in fields, trees were being felled in forests that covered the mountain, and lay there where they fell, flat, dead and sentient; claps of thunder sounded in the distance, shooting forth from a dark, sinking cloud that looked like it was about to explode. Elsewhere in the valley it was so silent that you could hear nothing but the twitter of birds; for we, too, children of all nations, kept quiet. It was a sunny day after an extended period of rain. Not damp, fresh weather, positively delightful! If only you were here. I felt your absence and kept thinking about you. I thought of Marwitz too; and whenever I witness the great outdoors which he so loved, appreciated so profoundly, I hope never to forget to cite his name wherever I can as a sign that we miss him, and that he is not dead and gone. Another downpour. One moment was indescribable; when we had descended from our ruins down into the valley, the scope of which seemed neither big nor small, the sun was no longer shining, except upon another ruin rearing up across from us, which by an optical illusion, was entirely ringed by our unilluminated valley: it was the evening itself. It loomed there before us, innocent, unrelated to anything else, impersonal, unoffended, without making any demands: it breathed in and out in perfect silence. Climb on! without future, it was simply there before us, unfettered, bathed in bliss. At the sight of it we all fell silent. If I could find a proper metric and the words to evoke what I perceive, I would make an enduring poem of it. When I got home, as soon as I stepped through the door, they handed me your letter.

I will follow hot on your heels

Frankfurt am Main, 5 September 1815
Tuesday, Midday, 1 p.m.

At this very moment, my dear August, I am in receipt of your letter of 30 October with Troxler's note in it, which I have not yet read; with tears in my eyes, I sit down at my desk to reply to your expression of love. I was already down on my knees to beg God that he should lead me to you. —One ought not to say such a thing!—ought not trouble God, although in all matters I am more beholden to His will than to my own— Listen, oh August, to what I've decided. On my honour! Under no conceivable circumstances will you go alone to Berlin, or wherever it may be, be it on a royal mission as a courier for the king, and even if that be the case, I will follow hot on your heels. These are our children, our bond, the fact that we stay together. That is what we live for, what we spend our money on, and what we contrive as a bond between us: you need it too badly, I suffer too much when we're apart. You will also surmise this from my most recent letters. I haven't written to you in several days, because I had nothing but uncertain things to report. I still have no steady company. But I do frequent

Delmar (from St Peter's Church), he and his wife are here, as is a sister of Madame Magnus, they are just waiting for a clerk from Berlin, who ought to arrive any minute now, to record their last will and testament; then they plan to travel with me on Friday; he insisted on not travelling via Brussels [. . .]; from now on you must know how, when and where I go to wherever I go. [. . .] Please be assured that I am glad to go to Berlin. On my word of honour, I swear it. And I'll come gladly, even if only for two weeks. It will likely extend into a longer stay. I am very confident about your, that is to say, our future destiny, even if it began under unfavourable circumstances.

Varnhagen, you must come out into the garden

(Remark noted by Karl August Varnhagen von Ense, 14 June 1823)

'Varnhagen! You must come out into the garden! You just won't believe the sight of the roses just now sprouting out of the ground! They have all reared upright in haste and in unison, as if responding to a sentinel's command!'

VI

REFLECTIONS

Throughout much of her life, Rahel kept a journal as a kind of letter to herself, a conceptual fishnet of sorts, a record of mind in which she jotted down stray impressions too private to communicate to her closest friends, yet too important to let slip.

I altogether lack grace

Berlin, mid-July 1800

I altogether lack grace; even the grace to appreciate just what it is that I lack; in addition to the fact that I am not beautiful, I likewise lack any inner grace. I have suspected this for quite some time now; but it is only recently that I became absolutely convinced of it; for far too long I noticed and only recognized individual manifestations of that gracelessness, as I often do with many things. I cannot say just why I do so, since I often find myself altogether innocent; I am lively and nimble, and value the same quality in others. But the bottom line is, I'm ugly. Once many years ago I said to Jettchen Mendelssohn, who was astonished by my words: 'I am unsightly.' So be it. There are some people who have no pleasing feature in the face, no praiseworthy proportion in the body, and nevertheless make a pleasing impression; they have downright unsightly features, and yet have something pleasant about them; it's the opposite with me, I might on close scrutiny be considered to have rather attractive features, and yet am not on the whole attractive. Come to think of it, I am not as unhappy about my lot as one might suppose; quite the contrary, this realization makes me feel at peace with myself. And yet I really do idolize physical beauty in others, really revere it. [. . .]

On being original

When someone says, 'You think it is an easy matter to be original! No, it demands a great effort; and it takes a lifetime of striving,' one would be inclined to consider such a person mad and refrain from asking any further questions. And yet that assertion is absolutely true, and quite simple to boot.

Every person would definitely be original, and necessarily so, if people did not almost always spit up prescribed sayings. [. . .] Thinking demands honesty, and there are definitely almost as few nitwits as there are geniuses.

An imbecile lacks the capacity for reflection, and a genius finds it so easy, on account of a fortuitous conjoining and accord of his personal qualities that it almost seems as if another being did the thinking for him.

Imbeciles would, of necessity, always be originals; but there are almost no real true simpletons; most simply don't have the reasoning capacity to be dishonest enough.

*No poet can conceive of a situation better, more varied
and extraordinary than what actually transpires in life*

28 November 1813

Just as no poet can conceive of a situation better, more varied
and extraordinary than what actually transpires in life, and
only an author endowed with the capacity to see the way things
really are, and to distinguish between the actual and the apparent, can write the best novel—so, too, must our most natural
desires remain raw, and their wilful fulfilment bring grief; only
that countenanced by God is in all respects beneficial for us,
because we can compose ourselves accordingly. I learnt this the
hard way.

History in the hands of madmen

Berlin, 3 November 1819

The time will come when national pride will be viewed much the same as we view narcissism and other vain conceits, and war will be viewed as mob brawls. The current state of affairs contradicts the fundamental tenets of our religion. Just so as not to acknowledge this contradiction, the most Godawful, insipid lies are told, printed and dramatized.

History in the hands of madmen can be very harmful and a fundamental failing deflecting its proper course; everywhere, from the highest to the lowest classes of society, there is a clamouring to question and study history. But who is knowl-edgeable enough to be able to write or read history? Most definitely only those who grasp the imperatives of the present! They alone have the capacity to resuscitate the past and to translate it, as it were, into the stuff of the present. Which is why Friedrich Schlegel's bon mot: 'The historian is an inverted prophet,' is so very true; and why Goethe is forever and always will be so great, so exhilarating and so lively: compre-hending and representing and explaining all eras, religions, standpoints, ecstasies and conditions. But those who read more history than they live for themselves always want to cite or have cited a version of life read in books [. . .] The desire to re-enact Roman history, with intermezzos from the life of Louis XIV, helped to topple Napoleon.

All mothers should be deemed innocent
and honoured as we honour Mary

Children born out of wedlock, not recognized as legitimate by the state, are commonly referred to as natural children, as in laws of nature vs laws of state. Children should only be identified with their mothers, and bear their names; and the mother should call the shots and hold sway over the family fortune: that is nature's way; the law should decree accordingly; any contravention of nature's way can lead to no good; how cruel nature can be, a woman can be abused, and be made against her will and inclination to bear a child. This terrible wrong must be rectified by human authorities and institutions: and laws must be made to affirm how much the child belongs to the woman who bore it. Jesus only has a mother. An ideal father should be constituted for all children, and all mothers should be held as innocent and honoured as we honour Mary.

Ever since childhood I have had a kind of horror of
clocks and of water confined in ponds and pots

Saturday, 21 April 1821

Ever since childhood I have had a kind of horror of clocks and of water enclosed in ponds and pots, barrels or casks; in short, of contained water. Only of late did it dawn on me that these are two different dimensions of the same dread, based on one and the same notion. Is it not odd that one can peer more deeply into oneself and sound one's depth in the dark without the illumination of consciousness than one can in broad daylight? In ponds and receptacles water's elemental will is checked, and its action obstructed; in the case of a clock an action is tapped. Which leads furthermore to the terrible conclusion that the released spring action is the germ of the organizational factor of telling time; if the reciprocal action of spring to cog were more versatile the contrivance would work better. It occurred to me today that a clock is the incipient organizational factor of the human endeavour. A comic application of force. [. . .]

Too bitter a taste is a true mortification

(Summer 1821)

[. . .] Too bitter a taste is a true mortification; too sweet an almost insipid, unendurable affect, a kind of mindless sense of wellbeing through the tongue. Sour engenders thoughtfulness; foments rumination. Saltiness has long been associated with spirit; and it enlivens, makes one circumspect. The mixture of these four flavours generates all tastes; it is the essence of pure wit. [. . .]

We talk a lot, because we cannot find the right words

Sunday, 15 August 1824

We talk a lot, because we cannot find the right words; if we could properly express ourselves, we would spit it all out in a single word.

We are nothing but drops of consciousness

(Record of a conversation, 24 April 1825)

In the small garden on Sunday morning, in the warmest spring weather, when the bushes were bursting in green; we had been talking about how we understand life, that one's own life seems strange, unfathomable in retrospect; that we only grasp it in the context of collective memory, recollected bursts of memory that linger before and after, outside the confines of an individual life; whereupon Rahel cried out in a burst of abysmal sadness: 'Heaven help us, we are nothing but drops of consciousness! I, too, long to spill back into the sea, with no particular need to be special!'

I am, after all, an ego created to accompany an I

Yes, of course, I am an egotist! I am, after all, an ego created to accompany an *I*.

What a despicable confession! And you're proud of it to boot?

It all depends on your interpretation: that is the basis of our understanding. The more tightly you encircle your *I* the more clumsily you constrain it, the more crudely you let it linger in direct indulgence, the more insufferable it becomes to other *I*'s, and above all the more burdensome to itself (in the deepest sense of the word burden); but to concede more clout to all other *I*'s than to one's own is a distortion or a calumny, at least in relation to oneself. So now do you better understand my despicableness?

Friday, 28 April 1825

To establish the nature of our consciousness
we must acknowledge multiple personalities

May 1825

We have read and heard for the longest time: 'A person does not know himself, the dumbest fool knows him better than he knows himself; if a person wants to know what he's like, he has to ask others, who see him as he really is.' I see the matter altogether differently. What kind of impression we make we can indeed only learn from others, including the dumbest and maddest of the lot; but what we really are like no one can know better than oneself [. . .] Let me reiterate: we see ourselves from a concave angle; others see us convexly. We also speak of entering a person's soul to judge him. But everyone sits inside himself. It is true that we are all the same, but only at the borders of self: inside ourselves we deploy, invent, contrive, conceive infinite variations on one and the same. Herein lies the greatest irony: to establish the nature of our consciousness we must acknowledge multiple personalities, that is to say a host of diverse selves.

Age is always unfair to youth

Morning, 5 a.m., 8 October 1825

Age is always unfair to youth; because age can know the state of mind of youth, but youth cannot know the same about age; and this discrepancy presupposes that youth already possess the distilled droplet of essential truth without ever having known the tree of life, whether leafy green, in blossom, or fruit-bearing. No swaddled baby can be any dumber and younger! Youth is pressured to believe age; that is precisely what it cannot do: the wrinkles of age are in and of themselves no certification of truth.

Age also manifests itself by dispelling the belief that we can accomplish or alter anything in the world. This insight promotes idleness; and we are actually still competent for much longer than we make use of our skills: life absolutely lacks new insights and discoveries; we come to the disproportionate number of our realizations and conclusions by our third year of life. Youth likewise has an advantage in that, conversely, the young remain convinced that they can accomplish, and especially, change much; and it is all too true that only actions effectuate change, that youth only really modifies the world; the inherited insights of the previous generations are laid down and cultivated in young minds; youth applies them afresh, and brings about new reversals. At the most, people function in top form on their own until age 40; after that, good luck willing, a person's insights kick in, that is to say, he convinces others to heed his insights.

We are a composite of fragments

11 December 1829

When we give a name to anything, we designate with that name one or more qualities of that thing, or none at all: but through its name we bethink ourselves by means of categorical memory of the entire thing. But what do we mean by the entire thing? Just the image of the sum total of the qualities of that thing. We have no language that can really convey the true essence of that thing; and when you come to think of it, we ourselves have no concept of an overarching quality; indeed, we are obliged to say overarching quality to even conceive of an approximation of an absolute. And that is why the notion of life is so often bandied about, because it is the only term that completely encompasses our sense of ourselves, albeit fragmented into various activities, and fathomed in temporal moments. We are a composite of fragments grasped while engaged in temporal tasks: tasks exploded into gestures—expelled from paradise; to facilitate understanding; immersed in a task in a part of our cognitive faculty: as here, when we momentarily lose ourselves in some inquiry. Of this I am quite certain: short of a stroke of magic—thinking about something does not spare us from the ordeal, nothing but total surrender helps—or play, in the broadest sense of the word [. . .]—but I am absolutely certain that we are here only contending with a part of our understanding of a thing: and this is solace and religion. It is not for naught that we are so divided, so fragmented in our thinking. Such fragmentation is regrettable, but there must surely be a good reason; as there is for all our follies. [. . .]

All that will one day be discovered is already here

All that will one day be discovered is already here: it just has to be recognized. What a terrifying notion! That all that is looming around me, that I live right in the middle of it, and can only encounter it as dreadful dead masses, and recognize nothing of what it will one day become. Even if I were to worry myself sick about it, the richest harvest of recognition would yield no more than it does now, for what remains behind is never-ending. —But the never-ending is not evident in the now—for what we already know likewise contains the eternal. That's life. Whoever fails to grasp this fact does not really live; but at least he feels that he's dying.

To grasp what we call life

To grasp what we call life, and what it actually is, does not, in fact, entail thinking of its beginning or its end; nor is it a matter of harvesting scattered sensations and combined intellectual and emotional insights. Children really live, as do others able to let life slip by—not the smugly self-satisfied and the braggarts, they don't live life at all; nor do those inclined to compile a clear picture of their accomplishments in preparation for burial. The fortunate few are those inclined to unequivocally contemplate the miracle of being, who study it each day anew without any preconceived notion, and better yet, those who retain a trace of their childhood sensations, for they have a solid grasp! And yet, how much do we weep at the death of an angelic child! [. . .]

10 a.m., Sunday, 30 December 1832

VII

APHORISMS

Rahel's letters and journals are replete with pithy pearls of wisdom that leap off the page, prefiguring the profound bon mots of Christian Lichtenberg, Mark Twain, Oscar Wilde, Gertrude Stein and Dorothy Parker.

Holiness

I have on occasion already conceived a notion of holiness; there were moments when I knew what it meant to be holy. Exalted above all change, absolutely pure, unattainable.

*

Nature has a thousand delights for those who seek them out and enter its temple with a warm heart.

*

Whoever does not tread around nature as in a temple will not find anything holy in it.

Knowledge and wisdom

Knowledge is a storeroom, a stock of reserves, knowledge is an intellectual holding.

*

We make no new discoveries, but it is always new people who make old discoveries.

*

A cultivated person is not one who treats nature in a wasteful way; a cultivated person is one who graciously, wisely and properly, and to the best of his ability, makes use of the gifts he has been given: one who fixes his gaze on what he's missing, and is able to acknowledge his flaws.

*

What else, in essence, is the human being but a question posed?

*

Our entire guiding principle is misguided. We make our youth wise, that is to say old. We rob them of the pleasure of self-discovery, annihilate their aspirations; what harm could it do if they're wrong? Those hopes never had are definitely dead! And actually, we just want to leave them less. Let her hope, but for the calamitous, which she could never wish for.

*

It takes 20 years for a human being to evolve from a plant-like state, in which he first takes shape in the stomach of his mother, and from the pure animal state of earliest childhood to that state in which maturity and reason begin to blossom. It took 30 centuries to attain a rudimentary knowledge of his structure, it would take eternity to know something about his soul. It only takes an instant to kill him.

Wellbeing and woe

The heart is the great clock that tells wellbeing and woe.

*

Pleasure! —Where does it reside? It sits in flower calyxes and emerges once each year as scent.

*

I won't let anyone say otherwise. Rapture can be found inside, outside, beside us, through us and without us.

*

All of my disappointments notwithstanding, my eternally mad spirit keeps hoping for the most incredible. We never give up on happiness.

*

Yesterday I felt myself to be in perfect harmony with all the things I know, and perfectly at peace with myself, and felt that this is the secret to true happiness; and in so doing, I felt my heart well up with the most complete, and at the same time resounding, reverberations of all life.

*

The fact that unhappiness is not a matter of conscious choice is what makes people so unnaturally, and so humanly, unhappy; but age definitely kicks in as a factor affecting how we respond when things rub us the wrong way. We no longer strive for the eternal, we take life in stride, and as they say, live for the moment. Tears, glamour and anger taper off in time; we become numb to offence, friendly, our face shrouded in wrinkles.

Love

What is often called love is nothing but a form of magnetism. It begins with an arduously ticklish confrontation, consists of a vilely divinatory sense of disorganization and ends with an odious clairvoyance and complete exhaustion. One of the two concerned persons generally remains level-headed.

*

Love does the heart good, a fact we immediately fathom when we are deprived of it. We live, as it were, in a cold spell common to all; often we don't know who in our proximity protects us from the chill until they absent themselves, and leave us exposed to the brunt of it, just as in a really cold room someone seated beside us gets up and goes.

Feeling and thinking

Logic is the art of determining the contours of possibility, in the rubric of which our head is capable of thinking.

*

Feeling is more subtle than thinking: thinking has the advantage of explaining itself, feeling cannot do so, and is our limit, we ourselves are the embodiment of that limit; it only knows that it exists. Everything can be defined by its limits; and the limits that no longer allow for anything else to surround our actual being, and consequently constitute the essential delimitation of the self.

*

It is just as difficult to budget one's feelings as it is to conserve one's other assets. One can with the aid of a lively imagination anticipate the natural outburst of ideas, such that when the future manifests itself as the present, one need only recapitulate the past, and is disconcerted to find oneself unruffled by things one had previously dreaded as the worst that could possibly happen. This we call being apathetic; and it is only a matter of mollifying misfortune.

*

Reason is the capacity—or better put—the rule in our mind, according to which, each time anew, we can reinvent the principle of understanding. That is to say: reason is a standard in us, not one that we establish, only in suffering do we take possession of it, it is already there; we only make use of it as a measure in our actions. It is extra-personal, a facility with which we are endowed that responds to us. It responds, for instance, to the question: How are we to react to incomprehensible things, to a miracle, as it were? To which reason replies: There must be an unknown principle according to which this, too, can be understood; thus, the purport of this as-yet-undiscovered principle has already been discovered; we only lack the intellectual tools to grasp it. The awareness of which fosters humility, speculation, etc.

*

Age comes suddenly upon us, and not little by little, as one might suppose; like every realization.

*

People are far too disinclined to say: I don't know; and if at all possible, they suspend their responsibility, hiding behind a word; so, for instance, they hide behind a notion of God or the like.

Lying and truthfulness

One lie usually already leads to the next.

*

We learn how to lie late in life, we are likewise late in learning how to tell the truth.

*

Lying is lovely if you do it of your own free will: it is an important expression of personal freedom. But it is degrading if you are compelled to tell untruths. If, however, you lie altogether unconsciously, you really make a fool of yourself.

The way we are

A stone can have a history, but only a creature endowed with consciousness can have a destiny. Most people just have a history.

*

We are actually the way we would like to be, and not the way we are.

*

And a bridge, a tree, a trip, a scent, a smile, in short, the entire superficies of life speaks to our ten healthy senses and our rich inner self.

*

The entire world is actually a tragic embarrassment.

Hope and despair

Do you know why we hope? We cannot live without pictures of the future. Without hoping, no prospect nourishes our will-power, in the absence of which there is nothing.

*

It is our purpose in life to have a clarity of spirit, and wherever possible, a pure, strong will. All that's left is to laugh, pray and cry.

*

Fertilize with despair, and you will yield a rich harvest; but the despair must be genuine.

*

Even statues from antiquity look like they could not live in the buff, as if they had only just been undressed.

*

Black slave trade, war, wedlock!—and still people wonder, and tinker with the truth.

*

I just wiled away a miserable morning. Still in bed. 'What are you doing?' 'Nothing. I just let life rain down on me.'

*

We almost never succeed at something that we do not later regret having succeeded at; and nothing goes amiss that we're not glad about after the fact.

*

You fling your failings like a shroud over my good qualities, and say that I am spineless. You want me to abide by only one premise, and that they call character.

*

I can forget what I haven't been given; but it is impossible to forget what befell me; God forbid lest anyone not grasp this!

*

As long as we do not also adjudge the injustices done to us that wring cold burning tears from our eyes as justifiable in someone else's eyes, we are doomed to endure the darkest night without any prospect of dawn.

*

If we were not betimes to allow ourselves to be fatuous, we would go mad. The civilities of the table at lunchtime—suppertime—saying good morning—the regularity of it protects us. Who has not felt his fatigue as a safeguard against frenzy: but not just because we are obliged to submit to sleep, I am convinced that even if nature were not structured such that we needed sleep, sleep would not suffice. We must know that sleep awaits us, that is what keeps us sane.

*

The malicious people are those who fail to respect in others what they prize in themselves.

*

In a social circle there can be no hierarchy; and any ranking based on love and on preference as criteria for special favoured status to enhance the pleasure of interaction must be painstakingly avoided. An analysis of the word *Gesellschaft* (society) should draw attention to this fact; it is a companion-ship established for shared congeniality or the like. There is no master, only a consort of equals; and no one can stand out as master. Consequently, kissing is so ludicrous or indecent at a social gathering. If all kiss it's ludicrous; if one kisses only one, it's indecent.

*

People's external appearance is the text of all that we can say about them.

Miscellaneous musings

Melody is torn harmony.

*

Everyone should keep a packed carriage and a dagger at their disposal for precipitous getaways, so that when fancy takes hold, they can promptly depart.

*

There is a crude way of criticizing by which nothing is gained, no one derives benefit, the only result is to dispense pain. But there is another spirited, well-intentioned way, whereby the criticized person is greatly benefited.

*

Concerning the matter of languages, our mothers and the languages called mother tongues have much in common. The former and the latter have children that marry in the country next door, and thereby alter their language and their customs. [. . .] The earth is covered with families each laying claim to nobility without knowing where they come from.

VIII

DREAMS

I am more wide awake when I sleep.

Throughout her life, Rahel mined her dreams, which she recorded in journals, for insights into her waking life.

Memorable dreams

July 1812

Now I want to record my reoccurring dreams in the order in which I dreamt them. Ten years ago, I stopped dreaming the first dream, which I had kept dreaming previously, over a period of six years, sometimes more often, sometimes less. I always found myself in an elegant palace, before the windows of which a lavish garden was laid out; directly in front of the building was a modest-sized terrace, and rearing nearby stood great linden and chestnut trees on an almost irregular grid, from which pathways radiated outwards to ponds, arbours and other shrubbery ordinarily planted in such gardens. The rooms of the building were always lit up, open, with a sizable staff forever in motion; I always saw an entire row of rooms open before me; in the room located farthest away from me there was a gathering of the poshest society, not one of whom I could picture approaching, even though I knew them all, belonged as they did to the same circle, and ought to have joined them. But this was impossible, despite the fact that the doors were open, and I saw them from the back ringed around a great big gaming table. I was held back by an inertia, a paralysis that seemed to hang in the room and in the illumination; I never wholly accepted this stoppage, and believed each time I tried to move that I was held back by other incidental factors; and each time I resolved anew to join the gathering in the distance. But each time, still six to eight rooms removed from the festivities, a creature I was unable to identify, since the likes of it did not exist in the world, blocked my way in the room I happened to be in; it resembled a slender sheep in height; pure and white like virgin snow; it was half sheep, half goat, with a coat of Angora wool; reddish brown at the snout, like the purest, most exquisite marble, the colour of aurora borealis, its paws of the same hew. I recognized this creature, though I could not recall wherefrom; it felt a boundless love for me, and was somehow able to express this profound affection, and to show it; I was obliged to treat it like a human being. It pressed my hands in its paws, which gesture touched me deeply; it eyed me with such profound love, the like of which I had never seen in a human eye; in a perfectly matter-of-fact manner it took me by the hand, and since I still wanted to join the gathering, we crossed the rooms together without ever reaching our destination; the creature regarded me with a gentle look, as if it had noteworthy reasons for keeping me from reaching my destination; but because I was determined to go there, it accompanied me out of love. It did so in the most extraordinary manner, namely, with its paws sunk, down to the second joint in the floor boards, through which I, too, could peer down at the floor below, even though the floorboards were firmly lodged in place; sometimes I, too, advanced in this way with the creature; sometimes on the ground floor, sometimes on the floor above, mostly downstairs. The servants took no notice of us, even though they saw us.

I called this loving darling my pet animal; and when I got there before it, I asked after it: since it had a powerful effect on me, too, and I cannot recall ever in my entire waking life to have felt such a powerful sensual feeling as the mere clasp of its paw had on me. But this was not the sole cause of my attachment to it; I also felt an overwhelming sympathy; and there was also the fact that I alone was cognizant that the creature was capable of love, speech, and that it had a human soul. But there was also something inexplicable, an attachment that in part derived from the fact that nobody but I could see or observe the creature; that it turned to no one else; that it appeared to conceal a profound secret; and that I had no idea where it was hiding and where it went when I did not see it. Nevertheless, this did not disconcert and upset me enough to make me pose any questions; and all in all, the creature's love captivated me, as did its apparent suffering, and the fact that by my mere presence I could make it so head-over-heels happy, which it always managed to express to me. Only sometimes, when it led me by the hand in that manner, and I fervently, tenderly pressed its paws, and we looked each other in the eye, was I suddenly frightened by the thought: how can you exchange such caresses with an animal: it is an animal, after all! But we kept right on as before; these encounters kept repeating themselves again and again with minor variations: namely, always in new dreams; in the same locale.

But I hadn't had this dream in quite some time; and when I dreamt it again for the first time after a long hiatus, everything was still the same, the castle, the room, the servants, the garden, the gathering; and I once again wanted to join them; there was somewhat more of a commotion, and a kind of disquiet in the rooms, but without any other disturbance or disorder; I did not immediately see my creature, which, it seemed to me, was often absent, and for a long time; a realization that neither upset nor disconcerted me, although I mentioned it to the house servants. Because the restive agitation bothered me more than the force that ordinarily held me back from reaching the last room, I climbed directly through the big glass picture window out onto the terrace, which soon opened into the open-ended piazza planted with trees; suspended there between the old trees brightly lit lanterns swung back and forth on big poles; I idly gazed at the lighted windows of the palace and the magnificently illuminated foliage; the servants scurried back and forth more often than before; they did not watch me, nor did I watch them. All of a sudden, I caught sight of my creature crouched down directly in front of the giant trunk of a tree, asleep on its belly, with its head hidden from view; it was black all over with a bristled coat of fur.

'My creature!' I cry out to the servants, who stop dead in their tracks with utensils in their hands and napkins slung over their shoulders, blocked in their advance, but not daring to draw near. 'My creature is back again. It's sleeping,' I say, and tap it with my fingertip to jounce it a little; but at that very same moment it kicks its legs in all directions, falls back down, and lies flat as an inanimate fur pelt, the rough side dry and the clean side grazing the ground. 'It's just a pelt, so it was already dead!' I cry.

The dream fades; and never again did I dream of the creature. —At this time, I was seeing Finckenstein, who was blond-haired, and after that Urquijo, who was dark-brown-, almost black-haired; if I were now to interpret the dream, which I did not do at the time: he bristled at me, and I found that he had no heart.

In my third dream, I found myself on the outermost rampart of a very formidable fortress, the expanse of which extended over a wide, flat, sandy plain far from where I stood. It was a bright, luminous midday; the sun shone so brightly that it engendered a kind of despair, since there is no refuge from it, no invigorating breeze, and there are no structures struck by the sun that might offer a soothing, green shadow. This weather had all the more of a pernicious effect since the entire region was devoid of vegetation and covered with arid sandstone that crumbled into sand; the surface was rough and uneven; the way places look where they dig for sand. This overly bright and blinding sunshine greatly irritated my eyes and nerves; and already worried me in and of itself. There was nothing to be seen in that godforsaken place; and it seemed as if the sun rushed by angrily, vexed at not being able to bypass this godforsaken place! So, I stood with my breast pressed against the edge of this old redout—in ruins, as was much else hereabouts—there was a crowd of people pressing up behind me; they were all dressed like Athenians. F. stood beside me, bare-headed, dressed like them, but in rose-coloured taffeta; without looking in the least bit ridiculous. I was to be hurled down off this bulwark, the outermost wall of the fortress, to the forbidding ground far below, among stones, limy sandpits, and altogether dilapidated fortifications and rubble. The people demanded my sacrifice; and cried out to F., who was their king, for him to give the OK for my execution! He stood there with an awful stubborn expression, and peered down into the depths; the crowd cried ever-more loudly and vociferously, and demanded that he give the go-ahead; pressing ever closer to me; they took hold of me, while keeping their eyes on F., grabbing me by my clothes; I tried to make eye contact with him, and kept screaming: 'You won't say "yes", will you?' They grabbed hold of me, flung me over the parapet; I fell from stone to stone, and when I was about to reach the bottom-most depth, I woke up.

Fourth dream: I lay on a wide couch, covered with a grey blanket. Opposite me on the same couch, without touching me, her feet likewise tucked in under the blanket, lay Bettina Brentano, and on Bettina's side, to her right, but to my left, lay the Mother of God, whose face, however, I could not see clearly; hovering over everything there was what appeared to be a gossamer, grey cloud, which did not keep one from seeing what lay below it, but looked, rather, like another kind of atmosphere. And yet it seemed to me as if the Mother of God bore the countenance of Frau Schleiermacher.

We were perched on the edge of the world. Far below us, to the right, directly beside the couch was a great strip of earth, somewhat like a big country road; looking minuscule from a distance, people ran back and forth and plied all trades; I cast fleeting glances and eyed them as one would something very familiar. We were the maids of the world and no longer resided among the living; or rather, we had separated from life—but it did not surprise me, or engender sadness, or make me ponder death [. . .]; but our business on this couch, that is to say our present occupation was to enquire of ourselves what we had suffered—thus a kind of confession!

So, for instance, we asked ourselves: Have you experienced personal insult; and if we had been afflicted with this suffering in life, we replied with an anguished cry: 'Yes! I know that,' and precisely this pain of which we were speaking tore a hundredfold at our hearts; but we were finally rid of it for good, and felt ourselves healed and light-hearted. The Mother of God remained silent, just said 'Yes!' and cried; Bettina asked: 'Do you know lovesickness?' Whimpering, as if howling, I cried out, with tears running down my cheeks, my face buried in a handkerchief, my lips exclaiming a long drawn-out 'Yes!'—'Do you know insult?'—'Yes!' I replied again, as before. 'Have you suffered injustice?'—'Yes!'—Do you know the pain of murdered youth?'—'Yes!' I whimper again in the same tone, and break down in tears.

We were finished, a load taken off our hearts, but mine was still filled with heavy gravity; I sit up, regard the women around me with upset, and want my heavy burden to be taken from me; in words spoken with difficulty, over-enunciated, so as here, too, to elicit a positive response, I ask: 'Do you know—*Shame?*' Both women step back as if in horror, yet with some sympathy in the gesture, they give each other a fleeting glance, and despite the narrow room, try to draw away from me. In a state bordering on madness, I cry out: 'I have done nothing! Nothing have I done. I am innocent!' The women believe me, this I can see by their lying still, no longer reluctant to listen, but they don't understand me any more. 'Oh, woe is me,' I cry in tears, that threaten to melt my heart. 'They don't understand me either. So, I will never be free! I must bear this heavy load;' that I knew. Forever! Merciful God! Oh, woe is me! Upset beside myself, as I was, I hastened to wake up. And even once awakened, the load still weighed on me, for I really do bear it in life; and if there were people who really understood my plaint, it would lighten my load. [. . .]

Music is God

Frankfurt am Main, 25 December 1815

Last night I dreamt I heard such a lovely prelude from on high, or from wherever it emanated, enough said, I saw nothing that could produce such perfect harmony, so that I felt compelled to fall to my knees, wept, prayed, and kept crying out: Did I not say so before, that music is God, the true music, whereby I meant that harmonies, not melodies, are the voice of God! The music became ever lovelier; I prayed, wept, and cried out ever more; as if in a flash, and without being able to put it into a coherent sequence of words, everything, all the being in my breast became bright and ever-more manifest; weeping tears of joy, my heart burst in two; and I woke up.

IX

LAST WORDS

In a sense, all of Rahel's letters and reflections, from her first to her last, read like rough drafts for a last will and testament. Between intermittent bouts of ill health, genuine psychic suffering and a lifelong brooding hypochondria, with an endearing frankness and a blend of earthy humour and matter-of-fact affect and an indomitable lust for life, every time she applied pen to paper she wrote as if there were no tomorrow, in perennial practice for her final exit. She, in fact, drafted two last wills in 1816, a day apart, and 17 years prior to her passing, the second being a personal appeal to her husband. She advises him, among other matters, to: 'Make haste to draft a testament! Every human being is forever dying.' He found these notes among her papers after her death. The betimes teasing, tongue-in-cheek, betimes dead serious tone disguises the fact that she was truly terrified at the thought of being buried alive, and so, insisted, among other stipulations, that she not be buried in the earth—just in case there be some mistake and she awaken from fitful slumber. These last letters also reveal a rare generosity of spirit. She requests that funds be set aside to care for two faithful servants, and insists, furthermore, that her husband not mourn too much. 'Do not shy away from starting a new life! And only dedicate to me that which you cannot take from me,' she solemnly advises. But there is nothing maudlin here. And to the last, she remained attuned to the sensory delights of life: 'I can still hear the organ grinder playing out in the courtyard, see the field out back, the sun in the sky; [. . .] I am absolutely at peace with myself; feeling downright jolly.' In 1831, already ailing, two years before her death, she found time to thank a former family cook for the gift of a roast goose breast.

Last will and testament

I felt so sick in Mannheim that I immediately resolved to put in writing what was to be done with all that I own and that over which it is mine to decide; and I decided to do so as soon as I could apply pen to paper without your looking on, dear August. In the meantime I told Dore how to dispose of a few small things, and I was well pleased to have done so; and felt prepared in body and mind for the moment of reckoning. That's how little I understand my hypochondriac inclination.

Varnhagen promised on his honour to fulfil my main wish; namely, to have me laid out without any fanfare in a second-rate coffin, not to be nailed shut, and with a lid that can easily be lifted: my casket lid should be made of glass, be it the flimsiest green panes, which I, in fact, desire. The casket itself is not to be buried in the earth, but set out in a little lodge—something on the order of a simple guardhouse of the kind to be found on construction sites—or else in an underground chamber, or some such place apart. It is my most ardent wish that, should I die after Varnhagen, whosoever of my siblings

---

Drafted on 23 April 1816, in Frankfurt am Main, this singular last will and testament addressed to Rahel's husband Karl August was found by him among her papers, and first read on 7 March 1833, the day of her death.

who does not follow my instructions will be my eternal bitter enemy!!!

I request that my piano be sent to my sister Rose! — Because she really loves me, plays herself, and saw me seated before the keyboard a hundred thousand times in the house in which we grew up; she attended my music lessons with a child's tears, and later with youthful tears, her heart full of desire and vague hope; in short, she followed my progress with every conceivable degree of anguish, joy, moodiness and thoughtfulness. It was while seated at this piano that I devised almost all my ideas. Should Rose die too, I bequeath it to Varnhagen.

I also possess a small emerald-and-pearl-studded ring; as long as my father lived, this was the only gift my mother ever gave me; when I was 16 years old, I saw it in the window of an English shop in Peermont; I had such a great hankering after it that my mother bought it for a half Louis d'or. In younger years I called it Wieland's pavement, as it seemed to be made of cobble- or garden flagstones of the sort found in his fairy tales. Later I contrived to stash it away, lest I lose it in the throes of boundless happiness—which at the time I did not conceive as an impossibility. Later still, I always became vexed whenever I wore it on my finger; realizing this, I lost the nerve to wear it, which I would otherwise have done, notwithstanding the sorry state of my hands; I ought to wear it all the more often, I thought, if I did not wish to be beholden to what the world thought of me; but over the years the ring never seemed meagre enough for such an experiment.

August, my dear, you know what this ring means to me! And if it did not seem childish of me, and were it not a gift of Mama's, I would not ask you to give it to Rose; but if you yourself have a hankering for it, you may keep it. My dear Hans, and my oldest sister-in-law likewise know how much I cherished it.

I also have a teensy-weensy ring with an uncut ruby and two small jewels: it was a gift from my father when I turned four, Markus got one too; I remember the moment. Markus let his ring fall from his finger in the nursery of our apartment, opposite the Rathaus, and it was never found again. Johanna and Fanny wore mine as children, as did Fritz Fromm. You can keep that one, my dear August; and let my gratitude, blessing, tribute, love and consolation stream forth for you!

—Divvy up the rest of my paltry, albeit beloved, jewellery as you see fit, August!

—Whoever loves me, let him care for Line—Line Brack, from Wusterhausen—she spent hundreds and hundreds of nights watching over and caring for me; and had to suffer all my youthful caprices and my moody ways! She forfeited her own health and youth caring for us. She served Papa like a faithful poodle, on bitter winter nights, and tirelessly attended to Mama; and you, too, Markus, caring for you in your sickness and in health, drawing your bath, attending to all your needs. Her failings, whatever they may be, are forgiven!— August and Markus, I ask you to care for her as long as she lives. I will come to speak of her again below, as I will of Dore.

—My savings, such as they are, hardly amount to a fortune, but can only serve to supplement any pressing needs. Conscience compels me to acknowledge that I owe it to you, August; but you will, I trust, gladly share the interest with Ludwig; and he will gladly accept it. He only has meagre means to live on, no money set aside; given his sense of freedom, a youth taken from him; and having remained at my side, and suffered through a terrible illness, and known spiritual terror, he merits our consideration.

Live well, dear Ludwig. My thoughts resemble yours on life and death, and evolved over time into a better and more beneficent attitude. Enjoy your leisure and nature, and bring me to mind in pleasant surroundings. Marwitz, Prince Louis, Mama, all are gone!

To you, my August, I need say no more. Having drawn strength from my life, I bid you delight in your own. Do your best. The less you give way to grief, the more it pleases me. I thank you, and love you, and honour you, and profoundly appreciate you, my dear one! Do not shy away from starting a new life! And only dedicate to me that which you cannot take from me. My beloved! My one and only! My true friend! I still have my wits about me. How wonderful! I can still hear the organ grinder playing out in the courtyard, see the field out back, the sun in the sky; and let my wishes in these pages be respected, as I respected those of Mama. I am absolutely at peace with myself; feeling downright jolly. [. . .]

Moritz Robert, may he have fun, and not take fright or grieve over me, he whom I love very much, and who knows how well I know him, and how alike we are, to him I bequeath my two mirrors with the golden frames: you can have them adjoined, together they ought to make a splendid whole.

—If you love and honour me, August, assemble in a packet and send my lady friend's letters back to her,* with heartfelt greetings from me. I remain forever her friend; have never held a grudge against her, even if I sometimes got angry. Let her not grieve, and brood over what she might still want to say to me: I accept and assume all good wishes here and now. People err, often jump the gun, and get stuck in their stubbornness; we all act too hastily. I embrace her in most tender friendship—

I also still have a Venetian necklace I had fashioned for myself. Let it be known of this object what it meant to me: a true sign of devotion to which I remained attached until my death.

God bless you all richly with peaceful thoughts and a profound feeling for nature. No need for a farewell! Adieu, adieu! Everything remains true.

Rahel Antonie Friedericke, etc.

My poor relations will all, I trust, receive additional allowances from Ludwig and August. Won't they?

---

* A reference to Pauline Wiesel.

*These words are but weak approximations and the
shadows of shadows of the life we've lived together*

Frankfurt am Main, 24 April 1816

Most precious, poor August!

If only I could comfort you when you read this! But I can
and do so herewith: through love and succour that still work
wonders; through the hundredfold talks we've had, through
the simple fact of our being and the role we've played in each
other's life; through being and nothingness. I was peacefully
and very happily engaged in drafting my last will and
testament, deciding what should become of my possessions
after my death. Here in the great sunny veil of Frankfurt, I feel
no more shaken than at any other time at the thought of
death. I did indeed shed copious tears when deciding what
should become of my old sofa; and of my string of pearls.
Papa was the first to die, causing me unending grief. In the
wake of his passing, I suffered all the illnesses, except for the
one that laid me low in Prague; all spiritual distress, all heartache; all perplexities and fear of life; all that remains of the

---

A letter to August Varnhagen von Ense never sent, found sealed, opened
and read by him on 7 March 1833.

sufferings of youth, everything, everything. The thought about the ring came to me at that dark moment when I was already dead certain as to my impending fate; that's when it became clear to me, that the ring resembled my innermost self. Innocent, young, of noble appearance and elegant and alone, and also as if enchanted, in complete solitude, and yet deep down joyous and polished to a shimmer, but always alone. Then I thought to myself: it will remain as an image and sign until I am no more. You know how freely and gladly I gave it: let there be no bitterness connected with it; you, my angel, my earthly angel, seemed to understand all that I felt for it, and gladly gave it back again to me. This ring elicits only praise, let there be no reproach or admonition associated with it. Absolutely: insofar as it was possible for a nature such as yours to grasp one such as mine, you have indeed done so; through your most astute, most spirited insight: magnificent, most brilliant recognition: with a perspicacity I find difficult to fathom, since it does not derive from a similarity of nature. Without a profoundly personal investment, brilliant deduction and insight, it is not possible for one person to absorb and attend to the essence of another, as you have done with me! No human nature has ever so whole-heartedly sounded the depth of another as you have mine! No one can better acknowledge this than can I; and such recognition could not possibly be enveloped by more love. These words are but weak approximations and the shadows of shadows of the life we've lived together, my ever faithful, beloved August!—Why then do I write them?—And what lies ahead in our life together!!!

I only wrote these lines to designate you in no uncertain terms as my heir [. . .] and as the recipient of half of my holdings, the other half of which I owe to no other living person, but which I ask you, out of love, to leave to Louis in recognition of his love and so long as he lives. [. . .]

Make haste to draft a testament! Every human being is forever dying. Please do so very soon out of respect for me. Do it right away! Live well, my beloved! May you receive God's best benediction. This is my purest prayer. Knowing you full well, I remain forever faithfully yours,

Rahel

PS The best that can be said is, after all, only that which best expresses what cannot be said.

The smoked goose breast is superb

(To Karoline Hübner, a former cook in her employ)

24 February 1831

Thank you so much for your kind gift. The smoked goose breast is superb! But my dear Karoline, you must not pass along the gifts you get to us; in any case, in a small town many things are harder to come by than here in the big city, so I really ought to send you something, not you us.

NOTES ON PERSONALITIES
Arranged alphabetically by last names

Maria Anna Adamberger (1752–1807), a Viennese ingenue best known for playing the roles of young women in comedies.

Bettina von Arnim, née Brentano (1785–1859), a longtime friend of Rahel, was a German writer, publisher, composer, singer, visual artist and illustrator, sister of German poet Clemens Brentano and wife of German writer Achim von Arnim.

Baroness Fanny von Arnstein, née Vögele Itzig (1758–1818), a Berlin-born Viennese Jewish salon hostess and wife of the Jewish banker and financier Baron Nathan Adam Arnstein or Arnsteiner (1748–1838). At one point, she was as well-connected in Vienna as Rahel was in Berlin, but, like Rahel, fell out of favour following the defeat of Napoleon.

Rose Asser, née Levin (1781–1853), Rahel's younger sister.

Susanne Elisabeth Bethmann (1763–1833), an acquaintance of Rahel, was married in 1780 to the Frankfurt merchant Johann Jakob Hollweg (1748–1808), who thereafter changed his name to Bethmann-Hollweg.

Georg Wilhelm Bokelmann (1779–1847), Danish merchant and diplomat based in Hamburg.

Wilhelmine von Boye, aka Johanna Hedwig Wilhelmine Countess von Sparre, née Hitzel Bernhard (1772–1839), a close friend since childhood and lifelong correspondent of Rahel's.

Line Brack, Rahel's servant and trusted chambermaid.

Auguste Henriette Elisabeth Brede, née Eulner (1782–1859), an actress based in Prague, whose acquaintance Rahel made in 1813, and with whom she engaged in an extensive exchange of letters that continued until Rahel's death.

Karl Gustav von Brinckmann (1764–1847), a Swedish and German poet and diplomat.

Henri de Campan (1784–1820), a French military judge based for a time in Berlin, a friend and correspondent of Rahel's.

Levin Markus Cohen (1723–90), Rahel's father, a jeweller, banker and businessman.

Dore, a trusted servant.

Baron Wilhelm Georg Friedrich Christian Heinrich von Egloffstein (1775–1859), an officer in the Prussian and Bavarian armies, a chamberlain at the court of Baden and a forestry superintendent in Bavaria.

Jettchen Ephraim, aka Rebekka, née Itzig (1763–1847), a childhood friend of Rahel's.

Baroness Cäcilie von Eskeles, née Zipperche Itzig (1760–1836), another prominent Viennese Jewish salon hostess.

Count Karl Friedrich Alexander Finck von Finckenstein (1772–1811), a Prussian diplomat and sometime lover of Rahel's.

Johann Friedrich Ferdinand Fleck (1757–1801), a noted German actor and director.

Friedrich de la Motte Fouqué (1777–1843), German Romantic author, novelist, playwright and publisher.

Regina Frohberg, née Rebecca Solomon, subsequent married names Saaling, Friedländer (1783–1850), German Jewish novelist and short-story writer.

Madame Gasparin, sister of Hieronimus Scholz.

Ottilie von Goethe, née Baroness von Pogwisch (1796–1872) German socialite and daughter-in-law of Johann Wolfgang von Goethe.

Ernestine Goldstücker, née Zadig, an acquaintance of Rahel's.

Joseph Haltern (1739–1818), a Berlin-based Jewish businessman, scholar by avocation, best known for his translations of works by French and German authors into Hebrew.

Antonie Theodora von Horn, née Graun (1782–1859), close friend of Rahel's.

Henriette Herz, née de Lemos (1764–1847), fellow Berlin salonière and longtime friend of Rahel's, known for her beauty and learning.

August Wilhelm Iffland (1759–1814), a German actor and play-wright.

Jean Paul, aka Johann Paul Friedrich Richter (1763–1825), German Romantic writer.

Heinrich von Kleist (1777–1811), writer and playwright, a friend and sometime frequenter of Rahel's salon, committed suicide by firing a bullet through his head on 21 November 1811.

David Ferdinand Koreff (1783–1851), a German physician and proponent of animal magnetism.

Chaie Levin, née Moses (1742–1809), Rahel's mother.

Friederike Auguste Liman, formerly Fradchen Liepmann, née Marcuse (1770–1844), a childhood friend of Rahel's and one of the very few people she addressed in German with the informal *du*.

Friedrich Ludwig Lindner (1772–1845), physician and writer.

Count Alexander zur Lippe (1776–1839), an early suitor and longtime acquaintance of Rahel's.

Prince Louis Ferdinand of Prussia (1772–1806), also known as the 'Prussian Apollo', military officer, composer and pianist, Pauline Wiesel's longtime lover and a friend and frequent guest at Rahel's salon.

Alexander von der Marwitz (1787–1814), Prussian army officer, friend and sometime correspondent of Rahel's.

Baroness Elisabeth von Münk, née Penckler (1753–1840), a guest at the home of the Arnsteins in Bade, near Vienna.

Konrad Engelbert Oelsner (1764–1828), German writer and diplomat.

Évariste de Parny (1753–1814), French poet.

August von Platen-Hallermünde (1796–1835), German poet and playwright. Offended by Heinrich Heine's mockery of the Orientalist penchant of his poetry, Platen retorted with an anti-Semitic slight in his play *The Romantic Oedipus* (1829), whereupon Heine struck back in *Travel Pictures III* (1829) with a snide allusion to Platen's homosexuality.

Princess Lucie von Pückler-Muskau, née Princess von Hardenberg-Reventlow (1776–1854), along with her husband Prince Hermann Ludwig Heinrich Hermann von Pückler-Muskau (1785–1871), were members of Rahel's inner circle of friends since 1828.

Friederike Robert, née Braun (1795–1832), wife of Rahel's brother Ludwig Robert.

Ludwig Robert-Tornow, born Liepmann Levin (1778–1832), Rahel's younger and beloved brother, a poet and playwright.

Markus Theodor Robert-Tornow, born Mordechai Levin (1772–1826), Rahel's oldest brother, the head of the household following their father's death.

Moritz Robert-Tornow, born Meyer Levin (1785–1846), Rahel's youngest brother.

Dorothea Friederike von Schlegel, née Brendel Mendelssohn (1764–1839), novelist and translator, best known for her translation of the work of Madame de Staël. Eldest daughter of the philosopher Moses Mendelssohn, she married and then divorced Jewish banker Simon Veit, converted to Christianity and married German poet and critic Karl Wilhelm Friedrich von Schlegel. She was a childhood friend of Rahel's.

Karl Wilhelm Friedrich von Schlegel (1772–1829), a German philosopher and critic.

Friedrich Schleiermacher (1768–1834), German theologian, philosopher and biblical scholar, and his wife, Henriette von Willich (1781–1840), were both friends of Rahel's.

Henrik Steffens (1773–1845), Norwegian German philosopher, scientist and poet.

Ludwig Tieck (1773–1853), German Romantic poet, author and translator and sometime frequenter of Rahel's Berlin salon.

Don Raphael d'Urquijo (1769–1839), secretary of the Spanish Legation in Prussia, was engaged to Rahel from 1801 to 1804.

Karl August Varnhagen von Ense (1785–1858), Rahel's husband.

Julie von Voss, Countess Ingenheim (1766–1789), mistress and later wife of Frederick William II, King of Prussia.

Arthur Wellesley (1769–1852), 1st Duke of Wellington, British Admiral and Field Marshall, best known for defeating Napoleon at the Battle of Waterloo.

Christoph Martin Wieland (1733–1813), German poet and writer, best known for having written the first coming-of-age novel.

Pauline Wiesel, née César, subsequent married names Vincent (1779–1848), one of Rahel's closest friends.